100 Years Of Altoona
From Coal To Cotton

Ryan M. Cole

Copyright © 2012

For information/inquiries contact Ryan Cole at:

8935 State Hwy. 132
Altoona, Al 35952
Phone: 256-295-4817
E-mail: rmcole@gmail.com

Published by:
Murphrees' Hill Publishing
http://mhpub.co.cc

Table Of Contents

Acknowledgements v

Introduction vii

Geography 8

Climate 11

Population Information 11

Pre-Altoona History 14

European Settlement 15

Roads 16

Early Coal Industry 20

The Man 25

The Company 26

Mining Methods 28

Other Mining Operations 42

The Commissary 43

Later Mining Activity 49

L&N Railroad 54

Culverts 55

Passenger Timetables 56

Altoona Depot 57

The Name 60

Building a Town 60

Governing Altoona 64

List Of Mayor, Aldermen and Town Officials 71

Businesses After 1908 76

Altoona Drug Store (Prince Drug Company) 79

History Of Hopper Telecommunications Company..81

First State Bank Of Altoona..83

Altoona's Post Office..87

Fraternal Orders-..90

First United Methodist Church...95

First Baptist Church..96

Second Baptist Church...98

Altoona Church Of God..99

East Side Baptist Church..99

School..100

Altoona Alumni...102

AHS Sports History...117

Football History..118

Appendix A: Altoona-Walnut Grove Cemetery..121

Appendix B: Altoona Cemetery..145

Bibliography...146

Acknowledgements

What a magical journey this has been. My love for the past goes back to my childhood, but my interest in Altoona history started in high school. I have to thank Andrew McCray. If it weren't for his persistence to hike up Altoona Mountain in search of a "bone bush", I would have never seen the rail track sticking up out of the ground. I also have to thank John Nix, David "Bean" Mitchell, Jonathan McCormick, and Brandon Taylor for the numerous times I took them on hikes and led them astray. It was through these hikes that questions were raised.

I must thank Danny Crownover and the Etowah County Historical Society. Danny was the first historian I found that actually helped me. He has encouraged me every step of the way and answered so many questions. The Etowah County Historical Society was the first place I presented my early Altoona research. This research soon became the basis for my book.

I also need to thank Mrs. Rhudy, Mr. Moss and the Blount County Historical Society. They have also been very supportive and helped provide several photographs.

A special thanks to everyone that I interviewed, emailed, and corresponded with. There are too many names to list and I fear I would leave someone out. Your generosity is appreciated more than you will ever know.

I must also thank my town, Altoona. I don't know how, but I ended up working with the museum as part of the 2008 Centennial Celebration. This provided me with hundreds of photographs and mounds of notes. It was because of this celebration, and the research that went into it, that I decided to write this book.

Lastly, I must thank my family. I really think mom and dad were skeptical at first, but their constant reminders once I started writing kept me on track. Thanks to my grandparents, Morris and Joan Payne, for the numerous times I sat in their living room going over photographs, to endless phone calls answering my questions. It's the persistence from my family and friends that kept this project alive. I want to thank all of you for believing in me. This book is as much yours and as it is mine.

Introduction

Has anyone tried to research Altoona or find simple facts about the town lately? Let me be the first to tell you how little there is about our beloved town. The purpose of this book is to provide facts and to tell the history of Altoona.

Every single piece of information contained in this book is from an original source; whether it is the newspaper, personal interviews, the 1989 reunion booklet, or other form of information. Whether a good story or bad, what I have compiled is true history. Listed in the bibliography is my list of sources, for which one (with a little research), can find all of the original articles or text that went into this book.

This book is a straightforward look at the history of the town. It doesn't include much biographical information about past government officials, townspeople, or merchants. With that said, where more in-depth information was available on specific businesses or churches I included it within the book.

The 1989 reunion booklet is a great source; however, it contained several mistakes and is outdated. This book is not meant in any way to replace the booklet, it is meant to compliment it. The 1989 booklet does contain more biographical and personal stories from the town. That is a perspective that I felt was well covered so I decided not to include it in this book.

I have taken great pride in reporting, as truthfully as possible, all that is contained in this book. Any omissions or misrepresentations were sincerely unintentional.

"The town of Altoona lays quiet and peaceful between two mountains, inside the valley they form." – G.L. Farabee

-Geography-

Geographically the town of Altoona lies between Altoona Mountain on the south and Parker/School House Hill on the north. Its border to the west is the Blount County line, and East Town to the east, encompassing a total of 3.81 square miles. However, the sphere of influence for Altoona extends northerly to Murphree's Valley, southerly to Warrior Valley, westerly to Tait's Gap, and easterly to Mountain Top. Altoona is 10 miles from Oneonta and 20 miles from Gadsden.

Altoona Circa 1950

The town itself sits in a valley roughly 925 feet above sea level at First Baptist Church, to its highest point of 1340 feet above sea level atop Altoona Mountain. The soil in the region is very fertile, and also very thin. One does not have to dig very far before they starts hitting chert and clay.

Within the town limits there are several place names and geographic features. Starting on the west, just outside of Etowah County is Trestle Road, off Highway 132. This section of town was once known as the No. 4 Camp. Continuing eastward, you would come across the train depot. South of the depot was the location of Altoona's first subdivision, the "Altoona Addition". North of the depot was the second subdivision, "Rickles Addition No. 2." The L&N Railroad Company built houses here for the employees who lived in Altoona: these houses became known as "section houses." Northeast of Rickles Addition No. 2 is Rickles Addition No. 1. North of town is the hill that Altoona High School was built upon. This hill went by several names. School House Hill is the name for the east side of the hill. When you go to the west, where College Street meets Valley Street, the hill takes the name Parker, Pink Thompson, or Shelton Hill. All three of these names have been used to describe this part of the hill. Encompassing this hill, from College Street east to the present location of the water tower and south to 5th Avenue is known as the "Ellison Addition." Everything south of the L&N railroad tracks within the city limits is known as the "Brown Addition." East of the Brown Addition is known East Town.

Venturing outside of town the first feature is Altoona Mountain, the divisional name given to Blount Mountain, which is a spur of Raccoon Mountain. Although it was disturbed by a century of mining, it still remains largely covered by trees of all kinds: pine, oak, ash, hickory, black walnut, buckeyes, gum, poplar and at one time chestnuts. Some of these oaks may be well over 100 years old. Although the mountain is not really known for having rocky outcroppings, it's likely that at the turn of the century before mining started, the mountain was indeed rocky. Examples of this can still be seen in places undisturbed by mining activity. Altoona Mountain is best known for its greatest resource: coal. This was noted by A.M. Gibson in his 1883 Report of Raccoon Mountain. He stated, *"Several seams, (on the back side of the mountain, north of Airport road in Blount county) are 12 to 14 inches thick, of first class coal. This seam is covered by a heavy bed of solid fissile slate, filled with very beautiful ferns. Every cleavage of the slate reveals these ferns."* Mr. Gibson continues, *"These beds are of great importance, as they can be easily mined and the coal can be readily carried into the valley through an adjacent gap."* The gap he speaks of is probably Drury Bynum/Maynor Gap. One of the most interesting finds from Altoona Mountain happens to be of prehistoric origin, as described in G.L. Farabee's *The Blessed Depression of the '30's*. Mr. Farabee writes, *"A piece of dinosaur was discovered in the mines. At one time the thought was to remove the mountain to preserve the petrified animal for a museum in Pennsylvania. After the opinion of a geologist who stayed in Altoona for several days, the verdict came down as 'too expensive.'"* From within the mountain comes several springs. The four most notable all form streams. One flows on the west side of East Town, the other flows just to the east of 10th avenue, and is also known as Kinchelow Creek. The third stream flows under Brown Street through the camps. These three streams converge where Lindsay Street and County Road 41 meet to create Whippoorwill Creek, which continues to Snead and empties into the Locust Fork River around Susan Moore. The fourth spring is the beginning of the Mining Pond Branch, also known as Terrapin Creek. It flows beside Trestle Road in Drury Bynum Gap, and continues north before converging into Whippoorwill Creek past Ellison's Crossroads.

West of the town on the south side of Highway 132, is small gap in the mountain named Drury Bynum Gap; however this present naming is incorrect as Drury Bynum Gap is one mile west. The correct name for this gap can be seen on the 1888 L&N map, where it is known as Hay's Gap. An alternate name for this feature is Bull Hollow.

Continuing west down Hwy. 132 for another mile is the actual Drury Bynum Gap also known as Maynor Gap. The gap is named for Mr. Drury Bynum who bought the property in 1854 and lived there as a farmer. The Maynor Gap naming, which can be used interchangeably with Drury Bynum Gap, came from John Thomas Maynor who owned the property presumably after the turn of the century. The spring that is present inside the gap is also named Maynor Spring. Here is an excerpt about Mr. Maynor and his wife by their grandson Eugene Maynor written in 1983: *"John Thomas and Molly Peddy Maynor lived on a farm about two miles south of Altoona, Alabama near what is still known as the Maynor Spring, in a beautiful valley near the foot of Straight Mountain. John was a Confederate Soldier, a staunch Democrat and a Primitive Baptist. Died in 1916."* Starting southwest behind the mountain and flowing through the gap and under Highway 132 is Hale Creek. It is also known as Drury Bynum Creek. The section before the gap and behind the mountain was dammed up in the early 1900's to form the Mining Pond.

North of the town is Murphree's Valley. It is named after Mr. Jesse Murphree, who settled with his family in the valley halfway between Oneonta and Walnut Grove around 1813. Also north of the town is the crossroads of County Road 41 and Murphree Valley Road. This crossing is known as Ellison's Crossroads. It is named after John R. Ellison who bought the property in 1858.

Venturing east of Altoona, the first feature is Vanzandt Hollow. Alternate spellings may be Vansant, Vanzant, or Van Zandt. It is unknown at what time the hollow acquired the name. The only record for a Vanzandt is a Mr. Geo. Vanzandt that owned a piece of property there in 1904. A Vanzandt Coal Co. did operate in the area, but it was not incorporated until 1924. The name first appears on the *1920 Birmingham Mineral District Railroad and Mine Map*, not as Vanzandt Hollow but as Vanzant's Altoona Coal Co. The earliest reference to the name Vanzandt comes from 1910 when the Altoona Coal and Iron Company leased the property. The deed reads as follows: *"All interested in a lease and leasehold of real estate (coal lands) located in Etowah County. ½ mile from west Altoona, being known as the Vanzandt Property..."* A letter was written to U.S. Geological Survey to see if they had any naming information on the Hollow, their response was, *"named on the U.S. Geological Survey 1:24,000 scale topographic map, and found by USGS field crews to be in predominant local use when mapping the area; we have no other information."* Continuing another half mile east of Vanzandt Hollow is the point of the mountain. This area is known as Pana. The earliest the Pana name is shown on a map is in the *1920 Birmingham Mineral District Railroad and Mine Map*. However, in the May 27, 1909 edition of *The Southern Democrat*, a reporter from Altoona writes, "Jim Wheat has moved a nice stock of goods from Pana (East Altoona) to Altoona." Dr. James P. Jolly wrote in *The Place Names of Calhoun & Etowah Counties, Alabama* that Pana was named because *"J.B. Pana and family lived here by 1870."* However, this is incorrect. Jacob Robbins and Jordan Thomas owned the property at this location during that time. Furthermore no record whether it be census or property associated with the name Pana and Altoona has ever been found. It is unknown why that area is named as Pana, although there are a few theories. One is that Pana was originally the name for East Town, as noted in the 1909 article. The location was confused during the years, and ended up becoming associated with its present point. The second theory is that the old road running from Walnut Grove to Ashville went over the mountain and through the location of Pana, which might suggest Pana was a small village. This, however, is unlikely since review of the land records from the area shows a sparse population.

The third theory has to do with the 1898 Pana, Illinois coal mine strike. The Chicago-Virden Coal Company attempted to break the strike by bringing in African-American miners from Alabama. After the strike, it seems possible that the miners could have come to work in the Altoona mines. They may have also brought the Pana name with them. Upon comparing this with the 1909 article, this third theory seems very probable. As we continue east we reach Warrior Valley and the Locust Fork River. It is unknown how the valley received its name; however one could connect the name with Native American origins.

-Climate-

Altoona has a humid subtropical climate that is characterized by hot summers, mild winters, and abundant rainfall. The average annual temperature is 62.3 °F. The average yearly rainfall in Altoona is about 58 inches, with March being the wettest month and October the driest. On average Altoona receives 1.9 inches of snowfall.

-Population Information-

Detailed population statistics were not available for Altoona, until 1910. Prior to 1900, what would be Altoona was divided between the Walnut Grove and Warrior Precinct. Using this information, it is estimated that Altoona had a population of 40-50 in early 1900. By the end of 1900, according to the Underwood Coal Co. payroll 36 people were in Altoona. Adding in families the population was probably close to 120. By 1902 the

Month	Avg. High	Avg. Low	Avg. Precip.	Rec. High	Rec. Low.
January	50°F	31°F	6.15in.	80°F 1.12.1949	-8°F 1.22.1985
February	55°F	34°F	5.18in.	83°F 2.14.1962	0°F 2.6.1996
March	63°F	41°F	6.30in.	87°F 3.20.1982	8°F 3.15.1993
April	71°F	47°F	5.25in.	92°F 4.19.1955	24°F 4.1.1987
May	78°F	56°F	4.78in	98°F 5.19.1962	32°F 5.2.1963
June	85°F	64°F	4.62in.	102°F 6.29.1952	40°F 6.1.1966
July	89°F	68°F	5.24in.	109°F 7.30.1952	48°F 7.16.1967
August	88°F	67°F	3.17in.	104°F 8.16.2007	50°F 8.23.1950
September	83°F	61°F	4.53in.	104°F 9.2.1951	32°F 9.30.1967
October	73°F	48°F	3.52in.	96°F 10.6.1954	20°F 10.30.1952
November	63°F	40°F	4.56in.	86°F 11.1.2000	2°F 11.25.1950
December	54°F	33°F	4.84in.	78°F 12.11.2007	-3°F 12.24.1989

Climate averages for Altoona

population had grown to around 500. By the time Altoona was counted in the first U.S. census, that number had doubled. Below is a chart for the census numbers through the years:

1910	1,071
1920	1,078
1930	1,098
1940	995
1950	860
1960	744
1970	781
1980	928
1990	960
2000	984

It is interesting to note that in 1916 the estimated population had swelled to 1,916. This was due to the increased demands for coal brought on by World War I. Another interesting fact is the population drop from 1930-1940. This is due to Gulf State Steel ending its mining operation. Detailed population statistics are almost nonexistent prior to 1970.

A breakdown of the 2010 census shows the following population information:

- 45.8% of the population was male, while 54.2% were female.

- 16.3% of the population was over the age of 65, while 7.5% were under 5, 76.2% of the population were over 18.

- There were 16 African American, two Native American, and 10 Hispanic residents.

- The average family size was 3.06.

- Out of over 426 total housing units, 220 of them were owned, 147 were rented, and 59 were vacant.

- In the 532 residents that were older than 25, 68.8% had a high school diploma to associates degree, while 9.4% had a bachelor's degree or higher.

- The average household income was $27,708, while the individual average was $18,472.

- 17% Of families were below the poverty level.

- The average home value was $68,600

View from atop Altoona Mountain looking north

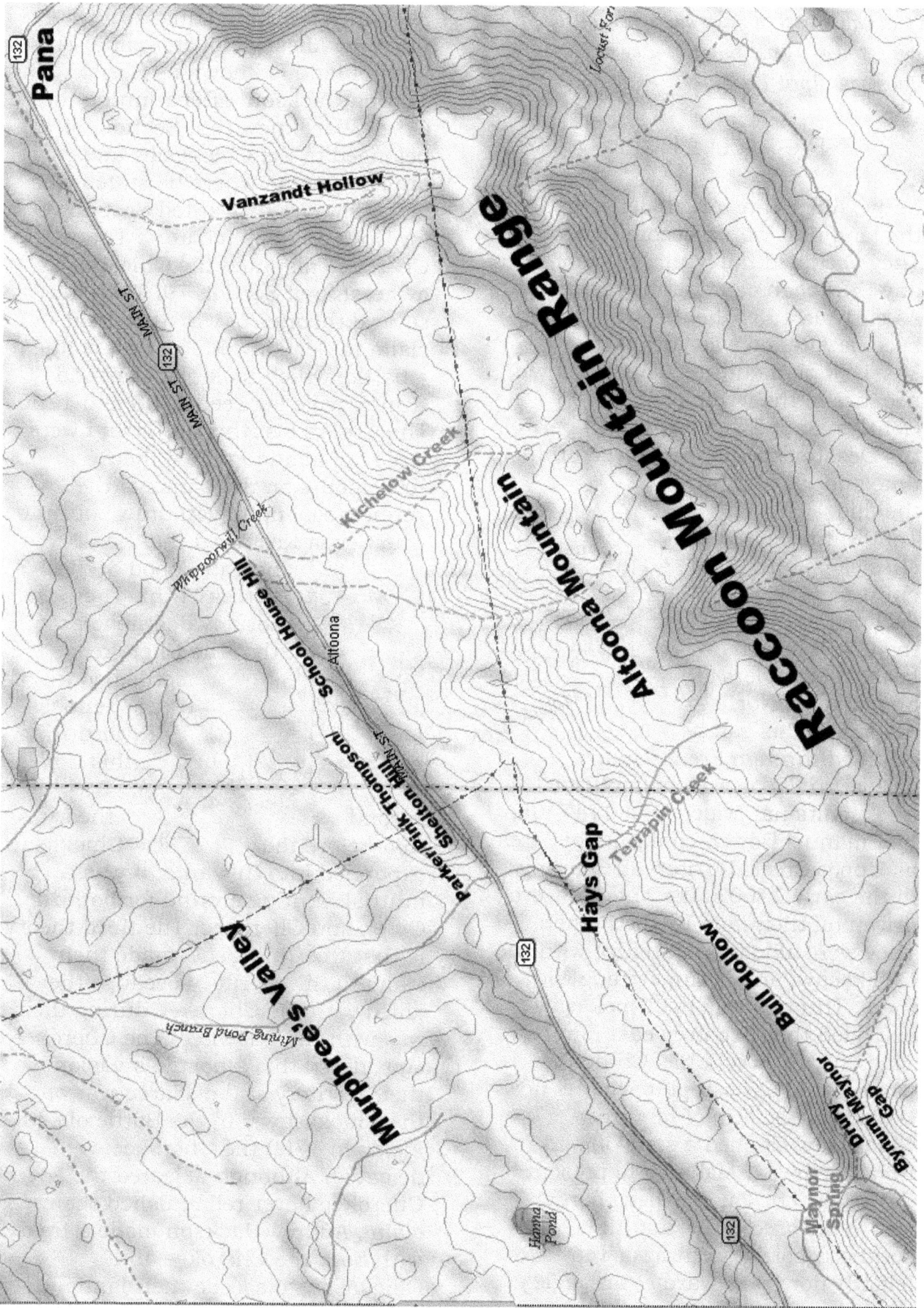

"Only about seven years ago where Altoona now is, was a vast forest." –Lewis M. Thomson, April 11, 1907

-Pre-Altoona History-

Native Americans originally settled the land that would become Altoona. They occupied the land well before any European came to the Americas. As early as 1539 the area that would become Altoona was part of the Mississippian culture. This is known because of the writings of The Gentleman of Elvas who was a part of the Desoto expedition. Between this time and the mid 1600's, the Mississippian culture declined and the Creek Indians became occupiers of almost all of North Alabama. This can be affirmed through French maps and journals, as well as linguistic and traditional evidence. A 1747 map by Emanuel Bowen confirms this area as Upper Creek Territory. Beginning in the early 1700's, the Natchez were driven off their land by the French. They were able to seek refuge with the Chickasaw, and began settling with them. Through this the Chickasaw extended their territory east into Alabama. In 1763 Chief Chinnabee came from Mississippi to what is now Gadsden. Because of him, the Chickasaw claimed a strip of land from northwest Alabama to present day Gadsden. The northern border was Tennessee River, and the southern border went from Ten Islands northwestward at an angle of 30°, until reaching Mingo on the Alabama Mississippi state line. This tract of land is known as Section 79. Andrew Jackson, after winning the Creek War, knew that Section 79 belonged to the Chickasaw and there are documents where he stated this fact. However he wanted Section 79 for United States territory. The Cherokee disputed the Chickasaw ownership of Section 79. There are several theories of why they held claim to Section 79. The first is due to a battle, which took place around Guntersville between 1700 and 1750. The Creeks lost this battle and were forced to abandon all of their settlements on the banks of the Tennessee, and to withdraw south to the Coosa River and the neighborhood of the "Creek Path". There is not any definitive proof that the Cherokee settled south of the Tennessee River during this time. The second theory is that before the Chickasaw expanded into this area, it was a mutual hunting ground for both the Creek and Cherokee. The third theory is that the Chickasaw made their claim to this territory because they allied with the Cherokee during their war with the Shawnee. The Cherokee considered this a hostile invasion of their territory and declared war on the Chickasaws. In the Battle of Old Fields in 1769 the Cherokee were defeated. Although defeated the Cherokee never relinquished their claim. Andrew Jackson made a treaty with both the Cherokee and Chickasaw to secede their lands to the U.S. government. The Cherokee signed the treaty on Mar. 22, 1816, and the Chickasaw signed it on Sept. 20, 1816. This officially removed their tribes from the land and allowed for land prospectors to come in and issue land grants to the area.

Today rarely anything is known about the Native Americans who lived in or around Altoona. Occasionally an arrowhead pops up but aside from that everything else is just legends and tales. One such story describes a large pile of rocks in a field off of County Road 42 near Harmony Church. The pile of rocks was said to be an Indian chief's grave. Another legend is that the tower or island on the middle of the chert pit off of Co. Hwy. 41 is another burial ground. Both of these claims are unsupported by any historical or archaeological evidence.

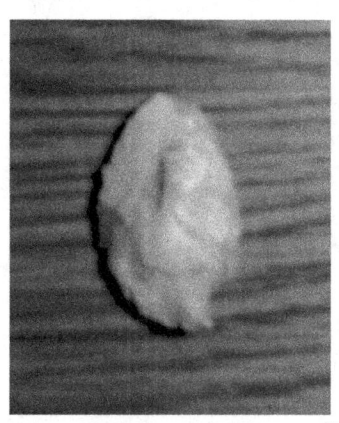

Arrowhead found on 10th Avenue

-European Settlement-

The first account of European settlement in the area around present day Altoona occurs in 1813. Mr. Jesse Murphree led his family to what is now Walnut Grove. However to west was a group of Native Americans. He had no desire to settle near them so he continued down the valley. Another group of natives were where Oneonta is presently located so he decided to settle halfway between the two groups. Soon after, Hal Cornelius and his family came to settle in what is now Walnut Grove (this has to be after the 1816 removal). Other early settlers include John Avery (1820) who settled west of Walnut Grove and Samuel Maverick (1921) who settled just past Ellison's Crossroads. It's important to remember the troubles these settlers had. The families had to pack their tools, salt, corn or meal, furniture, provisions, livestock, their wagons and the teams to draw them. It was not uncommon for horses to carry 200 lbs. on their backs from sun up to sun down. Almost all of the settlers were farmers and their main crop was corn. A bushel of corn in the Blount County area went for $4.00 in 1817. Adjusting for inflation that would be $53 a bushel today. In 1819 the U.S. government opened Section 79 and below for public land sales. The terms of the sale were in lots of 160 acres each ($320), one fourth of which to be paid down, and the remaining balance was to be paid in three installments. Because of the high price, at least two-thirds of these early settlers had no interest in owning the land they settled. Later a law authorized 40-acre land entries. This is why most land grants were not bought until the 1850's or 1860's.

After the Civil War the small community of Nix sprang up, located 2.25 miles southeast of Altoona. Not much is known of this small community prior to 1877. It likely consisted of a population less than 15 individuals. The community is named for Daniel Nix who returned to Alabama after being held prisoner during the Civil War. In April of 1879, Daniel Nix applied for a post office in the small community. This post office was most likely run out of Daniel Nix's own home. The community was situated very close to the Warrior River. Through this they had easy access to Ellison's/Harris Mill just 1,000 yards south of the village. By the turn of the century the population had grown to 28 and had three separate businesses. D.B. Bynum owned a general store, W.D. Moody Jr. owned a general store and Moody Manufacturing Company was the location of a druggist. By 1903, the post office now run by postmaster Dempsey Bynum and was situated at the junction of Moody's Chapel Road and Dee Nix Road. In 1906 the post office was moved 600 yards west of the previous location under the direction of postmaster James D. Moody. It remained at that location until the route was moved to the Altoona Post Office on March 28, 1907. The building at the last location was used for hay storage until sometime around the first World War.

Below is a list containing the postmasters of the Nix post office and the dates they dates served:

Daniel Nix	Jul. 23, 1879
W.J. Harris	Feb. 20, 1895
Thomas C. Silvey	Mar. 1899
Dempsey B. Bynum	Feb. 12, 1903
Moved to Altoona	Mar. 28, 1907

Another small settlement is Balm. It is first seen on the *1878 Land Survey Map of Alabama*. Balm is located half a mile east of Pine Grove Church on Highway 39. At that time it would have been halfway between the Murphree's Valley community and Walnut Grove. As far as any settlement in the area no population counts are known. Research has yielded two sources of businesses that operated in Balm. The first is a general store owned by J.A. Freeman in 1885. The second listing comes from *Dun's Regional Business Directory of Alabama*. It lists Balm as a banking town and the business listed is a general store owned by E.C. Bynum. This probably means that Balm was nothing more than a small settlement that acted as a local place for settlers to buy supplies and provisions. However a post office was first established on June 29, 1869. Below is a list containing the postmasters of the Balm Post Office and the dates they dates served:

James Thompson	Jun. 29, 1869
William H. Robinett	Sept. 11, 1871
Jackson T. Thompson	Aug. 28, 1876
Joseph B. Young	Dec. 26, 1882
Disbanded to Walnut Grove	Feb. 2, 1885
Reestablished as Balm	May 14, 1886
Mrs. Bettie Harris	May 14, 1886
James W. Dorsey	Apr. 9, 1895
James C. Waid	Oct. 12, 1899
Disbanded to Bird	Apr. 4, 1904

Although the post office was disbanded in 1904 the settlement continued on for two more years before it was removed from maps of the time. Several of the postmasters had very strong connections with Altoona. Joseph B. Young and James W. Dorsey are both buried at Altoona-Walnut Grove Cemetery. James C. Waid was one of Altoona's original councilmen in 1908. He was a member of the Masonic Lodge in Altoona and is also buried at Altoona-Walnut Grove Cemetery.

Hoppers Precinct is also a notable place prior to the creation of Altoona. Hoppers Precinct was located around the junction of Dee Nix and Nichols Road about three miles east of Altoona. The only reference to Hoppers Precinct comes from the 1877 Tallmans Map. It is likely that Hoppers Precinct was a small collection of families that lived in close proximity. Not much is known about this village. However it must have played enough importance to allow for a construction of a road through it. This road known as Hopper Road is also seen on the 1877 Tallmans Map. It connects to Warrior Valley Road on the east and follows the present Nichols Road, Dee Nix Road, Samuels Chapel Road, and Hwy. 132 before merging into what is now Hwy. 278. The only place that the road deviates is about one mile past Hoppers Precinct where it makes a U around McClusky's Mill.

Not much is known about McClusky's mill. Like Hoppers Precinct the only time it appears is on the 1877 Tallmans Map. We know from the 1870 U.S. Census that John and R.A McClusky as well as their eight children lived in the area. This is the last mention of this family, as they do not appear on the 1880 or 1890 census. McClusky's Mill wasn't as much of a settlement as it was a mill. The nearest mill would have been Ellison's Mill, four miles to the Southwest. McClusky's mill would have served all the residents of Hoppers Precinct and others nearby. The importance of the mill would also explain why the road went out of the way access it.

-Roads-

During the mid to late 19th century roads were very important for commerce, communication, and logistics. However, one must not view roads as how they exist today but how they were a century ago.

Early settlers coming into this part of Alabama would not have had any roads other than the occasional Indian trail. It was not until the mid-1800's that roads became more common in Alabama. These roads weren't stone or asphalt; they were just plain dirt paths. Almost all roads were eight or nine feet wide and just one lane. Sometimes roads were created out of animal trails or other sorts of walking paths that were simply convenient to convert into use as a road. Other times a road would be built over a route that offered ease of access, protection, or efficiency. Many times during large road constructions, engineers, and planners would be brought in to find the best route. This probably was not the case with the roads around Altoona. Instead as more and more people traversed a certain path it eventually evolved into a road.

Between the 1840's and mid-1870's, Walnut Grove had three roads that connected it to Murphree's Valley, Aroura, Bennettsville, and Blountsville. However there was not a direct route to Ashville. If one wanted to go to Ashville they would have to travel east to Gadsden or west to Oneonta. In 1868 the Alabama and Chattanooga Railroad began operating through Ashville and Steele. This railroad must have prompted residents to build a road leading out of Walnut Grove to Ashville. This road is known as "Walnut Grove Road." It is first found on the 1877 Tallmans Map of Etowah County. On this 1877 map Walnut Grove Road starts where present day Nichols Road meets Warrior Valley Road. From there it

Millstone

runs north and connects to what is now known as Thompson Road. However the road did not follow the current route of Warrior Valley Road around the mountain. Instead, Walnut Grove Road goes over the mountain. This road would have run directly through what would later be known as Pana. It is not known if Pana had any settlement or place of business at all during this time. By 1893, Warrior Valley Road as we know it now was completed and what would become Hwy. 132 was also built. However, the route over the mountain is still shown. These three roads converge at one point: Pana. This furthers speculation that Pana was some sort of settlement during this time period.

This is the last time Walnut Grove Road is mentioned on a map. As stated before Pana is not mentioned on a map until 1915. The only mention we have of Pana outside of a map is from the May 27, 1909 edition of the *Southern Democrat*. In an article written by an Altoona Reporter that states, *"Jim Wheat has moved a nice stock of goods from Pana (East Altoona) to Altoona."* This fact confirms that there was a business of some kind at Pana (or East Town) between 1905 and 1909.

Another thing to look at is that by 1893 there was a road leading east-west from Pana through what would become Altoona. This road can first be seen on the 1885 topographical map. The road runs from Pana down the current Highway 132, turns right at 12th Avenue, and makes a U, onto the current County Highway 41, then left again onto Highland Street and converges back onto the current Highway 132 at the Blount county line. This road

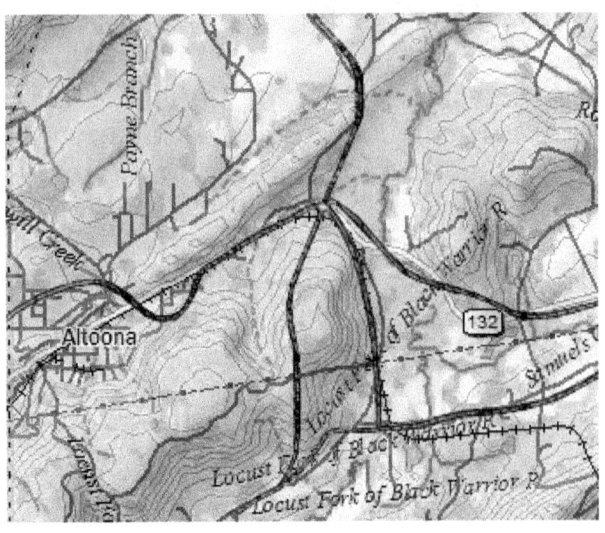

1893 Map superimposed on a modern day map

continued east down Highway 132 in which it curved north, down the current Hale Creek Road until meeting up with Murphree's Valley Road. This road shows that in the eight-year period since the Tallmans Map, a need to build an easterly route from Pana was justified. This was all due to one thing: coal. That resource would soon transform the quiet countryside into a bustling town.

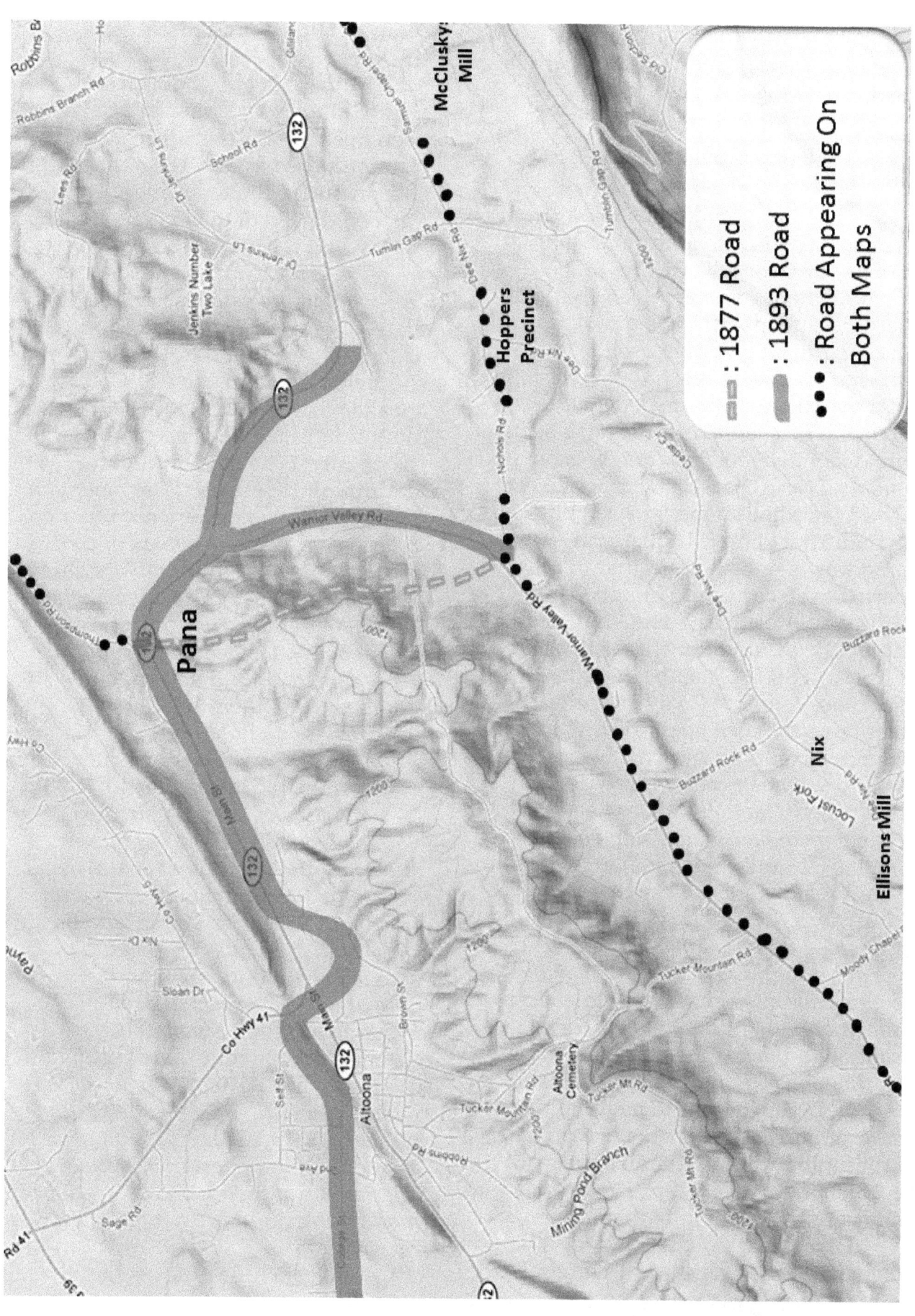

"The Coal is of superior quality, abundant in quantity and easily worked." – The Southern Democrat, October 11, 1900

-Early Coal Industry-

The first mention of coal is from *A History and Description of Blount County* by George Powell in 1855. Here he mentions the region that will become Altoona. *"This is a coal region and nearly all of it composed of mountains. It is in this narrow division that the Locust Fork has its main source. The coal beds that I have seen are about two feet thick and of good quality."* Note that this was before the Civil War when Alabama was still an agricultural center. Industry in the area was lagging behind that of other parts of the country. Thus the coal beds would primarily remain untouched until after the Civil War.

In 1883 A.M. Gibson wrote *The Raccoon Mountain Coal Field,* in it he mentions the coal fields around what would encompass Altoona. He states, *"Many seams of coal are exposed in this region. Enough coal for home consumption is conveniently gotten from the beds of the streams, and hence it has not been sought for elsewhere. Those seams that have withstood denudation are generally the harder and thinner seams, while the softer and thicker out-crops have been swept away. The out-crops of these softer and thicker seams can be found on the higher grounds on the sides of the hills."* He goes on to mention several mines that are opened on this seam. (The following mine names correspond to the figure 1 map showing the location of these mines.)

Mine 1 is noted as being opened but not yet in use. The coal seam at Mine 1 is four feet in thickness.

Mine 2 is about 800 feet to the east of Mine 1 and was said to have been opened and mined in the past but not in use by the 1883 report. Mr. Gibson states the following, *"From this bed a good deal of very excellent coal is said to have been taken."*

In 1891 Eugene Gibson wrote *"A report on the coal measures of the Plateau Region of Alabama."* In it he described several other mines. In the chapter devoted to Etowah County he speaks of the coal within the mountain in the southwest corner of the county, (The coal of Altoona Mountain). He states, *"The mountain is very broken and there are reported to be from four to six seams of coal exposed. These coal seams are said to range in thickness from a few inches to four feet."* Later he continues, *"These coal seams have been dug in but a very few places and so very little is known as to their true number, thickness and quality."*

He also speaks about new mines since his last report in 1883. *"A seam was opened by Mr. Zach. Payne. It showed eight feet of solid and apparently excellent coal. This is known as the Payne bed. Another opening nearby has been made by Mr. G.F. Gaither. At this opening the coal seam measured four feet and appeared to be excellent coal. It is known as the Smith bed."* Later he talks about more testing on the mountain. *"The Alabama State Land Company, which owns a large portion of this field, has had a good deal of testing done in many places. The results of their work have not been made public, and are not generally available."*

He concludes the section by

paying a compliment to the coal found in this section of the mountain. *"The coal from all these openings have gained a high reputation as a shop coal. It is said to be very free from sulfur and to coke well and easily. This seam of coal is probably the best yet opened in the field. It is also the highest known seam, and is formed only on the highest points of the mountain."*

The last report made by A.M. Gibson was in 1893 and entitled *The Coal Measures of Blount Mountain*. This report was more detailed then the preceding reports. This was due to surveys done by the Alabama Geological Survey between 1891 and 1892. It was expressed by citizens of the area that, *"more coal has been developed in one season by the Geological Survey than has been done by all preceding prospectors."*

The first new mine he refers to is labeled as mine 1A. Mr. Gibson writes, *"This opening was made many years ago, and coal was taken out from time to time by many different parties. The opening was made by sinking pit in a flat hollow, near the side of a branch, and below water level. Many statements, probably exaggerated, were made about the thickness of this seam by the parties who had dug coal here. They generally agreed that the seam was over 'six feet thick.' These statements were made by men of average intelligence and unquestioned veracity."* Later Mr. Gibson continues, *"This is a very remarkable seam of coal-practically it carries no sulfur. It will be largely utilized in the future for smelting iron and furnace work."*

The next few pages of the report cover the previously mentioned Smith and Paine beds. *"These seams are better known than any other in this coal field. They are the only one on which coal mining to supply the market has successfully been carried on."*

A mine by G.B. Carnes is mentioned next, *"A tunnel was driven in by G.B. Carnes, who supplied the local demand for coal for several years."*

Samuel Smith is mentioned as uncovering a seam of coal, but mining had not started at that time.

He then expands on the G.F. Gaither mine he mentioned in his 1891 report. *"A wide opening has been made, and the coal is said to be four feet thick, and of very good quality."*

By 1893 Mr. Gaither has made a second opening (Gaither #2) to the northwest. The coal here is described as being three feet thick.

James Smith owns the next mine mentioned. Mr. Gaither writes that the mine saying, *"The coal has a fine reputation, and there is a ready home market for all that has yet been mined here. The coal is three feet thick."*

James Smith has another mine northeast of the Warrior River, but it was said that this prospect *"was not so good"*.
Going back and reviewing the information contained in these reports it's possible see the development of the coal industry in what would become Altoona.

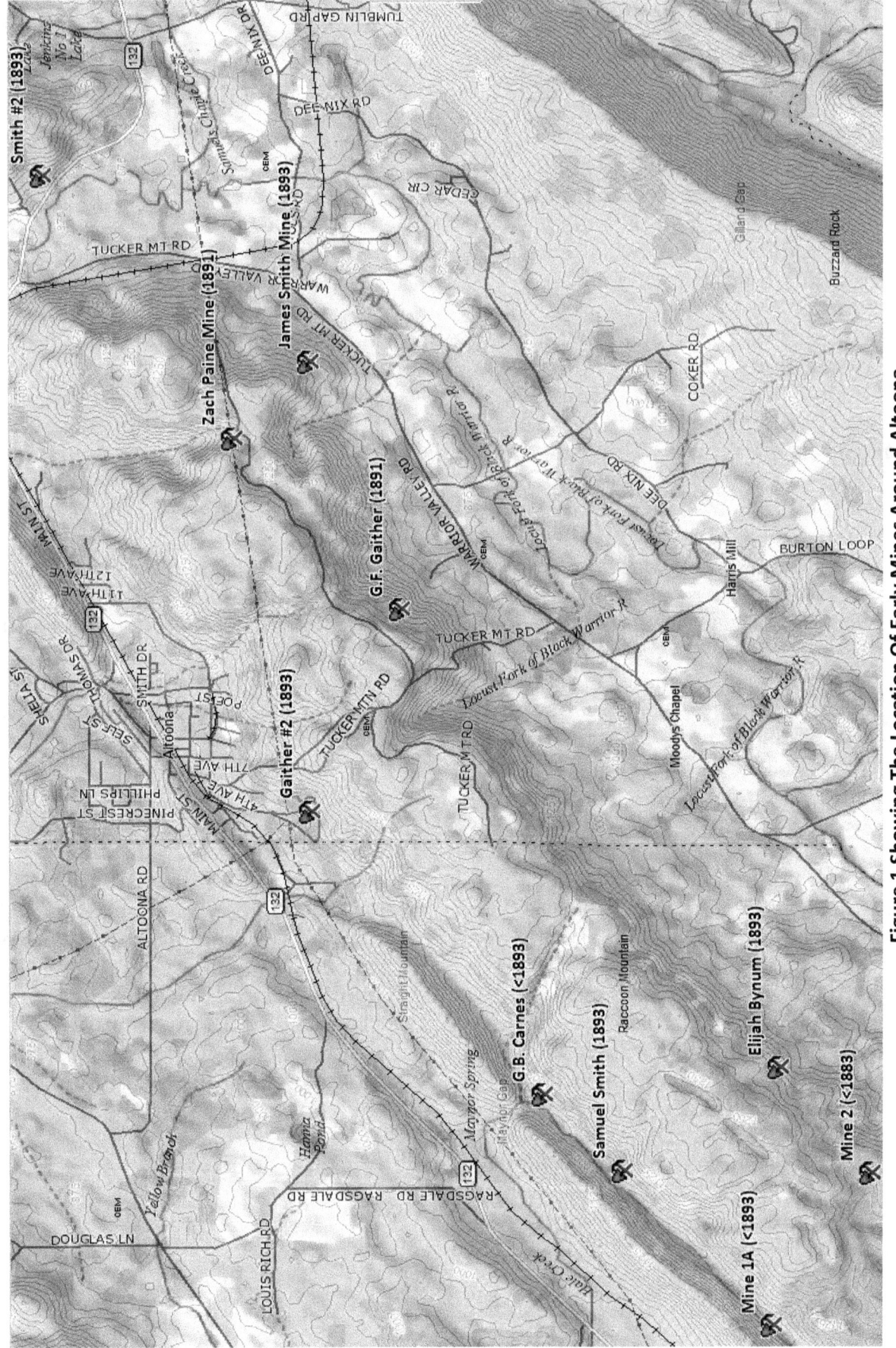

Figure 1 Showing The Location Of Early Mines Around Altoona

All three reports do not mention any kind of extensive industrial mining. All of the mines are owned and operated by local individuals. As noted in the 1883 report coal was being pulled from exposed seams and used to heat homes. This coal was probably sold in the general stores and used in the homes of Walnut Grove, Balm, and Nix. At this time there are two different mines present. Mine 2 is noted as being mined in the past; this is probably the first mine in the Altoona area. By the 1891 report several more mines had opened and the L&N Railroad as well as the Alabama State Land Company were conducting tests. In this report more details are given and it is mentioned that the coal is known as a good shop coal. This statement leads one to believe that the focus is shifting from consumer to industrial use. Apparently great interest was taken in the area as the Alabama Geological Survey conducted an extensive survey and Mr. Gibson published his third and most detailed report on the mountain. He mentions Mine 1A, which could be Mine 2 mentioned in the previous report, although the location is several hundred yards off. He also notes his amazement of the coal quality from this mine and foreshadows the industry that would come to the area. He continues to give details of other new mines that have opened as well as updating the status of mines mentioned in previous reports.

It's also important to examine the methods these early miners used. Examination of the census records for the time tells the following.

Samuel Smith was 50 at the time and his occupation is listed as a farmer.

Elijah Bynum was 59 and was also a farmer.

G.F. Gaither was 39 and a farmer.

Zach Payne was 43 and a farmer.

G.B. Carnes was 42 and his occupation was a blacksmith.

No record could be found for James Smith.

At the time one ton of coal was only worth about $1.00. They didn't mine the coal as it is mined today mining it. Instead they probably dug it out of the top of the ground, where seams were exposed. When deeper digging was required, they most likely used picks and horse drawn shovels to dig down a few feet. These men never had a drift or shaft mine. Instead they probably loaded their coal onto mule drawn wagons and used it to heat their homes or to sell to locals to make some extra money.

Example of small scale above ground mining

The lone exception to this method would be G.B. Carnes. He was a blacksmith and his mine reflects that. His mine was a tunnel although no exact details were given. It was most likely the first drift mine to operate in the area. It is still doubtful that he used powder to blast the coal out. Instead his tunnel was probably made by hand picking rock and coal away and using wood as an abutment. As a blacksmith his use of coal was more than that of a farmer. From the description it seems he may have also sold some of the coal from his mine.

All of these men mined this coal for their personal or local use. Mr. Gibson foreshadowed the future with one of his last lines in his 1893 report, *"Only the great industrial developments of the future will fully expose this important coal field."*

Example of a drift mine

"Mr. W.T. Underwood, President of the Underwood Coal Co. extended to the people a warm and cordial welcome that made each and every one feel at home. All were impressed with the sincerity, earnestness, and good taste of the hearty greeting." – The Southern Democrat, July 10, 1902

-The Man-

William Thompson Underwood was born on July 24, 1848 at Nashville, Tennessee. He was the son of Eugene and Katherine (Thompson) Underwood. Mr. Underwood's father was one of the pioneer officers of the Louisville & Nashville railroad and a lawyer. Mr. W.T. Underwood was raised in Kentucky and he received his education in the public schools of Louisville and the Forest Academy. He began to study law early and was admitted to practice in the Kentucky courts. He later found his way to the northwest led by land deals and speculation. While in Minnesota he met and married his Marinda Burnett Wilder on October 4, 1871, in St. Paul. They had three children. By 1882 he made his way south and settled in Birmingham. In 1883, Mr. Underwood and Henry F. DeBardeleben formed their own company and opened the Mary Pratt furnace. In 1884 they leased a tract of ore land from the Alice Furnace Company on Red Mountain and opened the Reading Mines. In 1890 Mr. Underwood dissolved the Mary Pratt Company. In 1898 Mr. Underwood formed a partnership under the firm name of Garrett, Underwood and Thach. Mr. Underwood was also a director of the First National Bank and the Birmingham Trust and Savings Company. He was a Democrat, a member of the Episcopal Church, and a Knight Templar. Mr. Underwood died on Jun. 27, 1916 and was buried at Oak Hill Cemetery in Birmingham. His body was later moved to Louisville, Kentucky on July 7, 1916.

The following article titled *Altoona's Founder* by Osgood Taylor appeared in the Oct. 26, 1905 edition of the *Southern Democrat*.

The father of our hero was a thoroughbred Kentuckian and Kentucky produces the finest horses, mules and the prettiest women and the most magnificent men. The father of the subject of this sketch was also one of the original stockholders of the L&N R.R. W.T. Underwood, whose mastermind conceived and started the Altoona mines, was the son of Eugene Underwood, a gifted Kentucky lawyer and railroad stockholder, was born July 24th, 1848, at Nashville, Tenn., but was carried in boyhood back to Kentucky and entered school at Bowling Green at the age of ten years, and afterward he attended the city schools at Louisville and Forest Academy. When of age he was admitted to the bar and practiced law successfully in Louisville, Ky., and while at San Antonio, Texas, where he had gone to look into some land titles for a Kentucky client, he met Henry F. DeBardeleben, who was also out west at the time, and who induced W.T. Underwood to come to Birmingham to build a blast furnace and open mines. Since that time Capt. W.T. Underwood has been making iron, operating mines, prospecting, examining mineral properties, making expert reports on them, dealing in real estate connected therewith and to. He brought his family to Birmingham in the spring of 1882, and settled on the South Highlands, where he still resides. Capt. Underwood is indeed a remarkable man. In business he is shrewd and able; discreet in all things to a golden silence. His nice manners bespeak the gentle man he is while his well-poised head and clear eyes tell of a great soul within. I like his friendly greetings, for when you meet him he always speaks first and I have seen him stop and sit down by the way-side to listen kindly to a statement from the dirtiest man on the job. Capt. Underwood made Altoona what it is today. And our school building of which we are proud, is a monument to his generosity. He was reared in Kentucky where many capable men saw the light in those good old homes antedating the "Lost Cause." Henry Waterson expressed it best when he said, "The fire burns bright in the old Kentucky home tonight."

-The Company-

Tradition says that Mr. Underwood came into what would become Altoona in February 1900. While this is probably true the first record is from the incorporation date of May 11, 1900. He purchased approximately 2,280 acres including what is now downtown Altoona. Most of that original property he bought from J.N. Rickles. In 1902 he added 900 acres west of Altoona on the mountain. Underwood Coal Company was created with W.T. Underwood as President, James G. Garrett as chair, Robert H. Thatch as Secretary (also received subscriptions and stock), C. Fuller Mauley also as a Secretary, and W.T. Underwood as Treasurer. The company was incorporated with a capital stock of $50,000

Col. James J. Garrett was a leading lawyer in Birmingham, Alabama. He was born in North Carolina in 1837. His parents moved to Greene County Alabama a year later. He was educated at the University of Alabama and was later admitted to the bar. He joined the Confederacy in the Civil War and was promoted to the rank of colonel. It was during this time he was assigned to duty at General Lee's headquarters. He returned to Alabama after the war where he continued to practice law. Col. Garrett was twice mayor of Greensboro, Alabama. In 1898 he was a forming partner in the firm Garrett, Underwood and Thach. However in 1902 he retired.

Robert H. Thach was born in Alabama on Nov. 9, 1866. He was educated at the Alabama Polytechnic Institute and graduated in 1885. He then taught higher mathematics at Marvin College in Clinton, Ky. In 1886 he went to Europe and was vice-consul at St. Etienne, France for over two years. While in this position he traveled Europe and studied law. Upon returning to the United States he relocated to Birmingham and was admitted to the bar. Mr. Thach later was a founding member of the firm Garrett, Underwood and Thach. He was an avid politician and was elected as an alderman in Birmingham in May 1901.

The Blount County News Dispatch first mentions Mr. Underwood in a May 17, 1900 article: *Mr. Underwood who is to operate the mines eight miles east of Oneonta, was in town a few days ago. He will soon erect seventy-five houses and a commissary. About 800 hands will be employed. This new mine is on the of the railroad recently erected from Oneonta and Attalla. The final survey of this road is now being made and grading will begin in a few days.* Some time passed before any new news was reported on the mines. However the October 11, 1900 edition of the *Blount County News Dispatch* states, *"Mr. Underwood has a contract to furnish 50,000 tons of coal to the Louisville and Nashville railroad. The coal miners are making good money. Men who have little or no experience in mining make from $50 to $65 per month. Operations have not fairly begun there, yet Mr. Underwood's pay roll for last month amounted to over $2,000".*

Soon after mining began about 200 men, mined an estimated 6,700 tons of coal each month. The company continued to expand and grow. These original mines were about a mile inside Blount County and were known as the "Underwood Drifts." The next mention of the company comes from a July 5, 1904 article in the *Attalla Mirror*. The article is titled "Altoona Miners will not strike." It reads, *"A telephone message was received from a party at Altoona on Friday last stating that the miners at work in the underwood coal mines would not strike. The miners and mine owners have affected an arrangement by which the miners are to work on without any loss of time until the scale question is settled. The big mines at Altoona have been worked by a large force of miners all the time during the past year.*

At present extensive improvements are being made at the mines and many new rooms are being opened in the present mines. This means that a large number of miners will be put on soon. The intention of the company is to largely increase the output of their mines as soon as the new road is completed, and for this reason the new rooms are now being opened, so they will be ready for the new miners at the time stated."

The next article jumps ahead to December 2, 1905 where it is first mentioned about a merger of Underwood Coal Company into the Southern Steel Company. This merger was not mentioned again until December 8. The following is an excerpt from that article in the *Gadsden Times:*

Brick from the Southern Steel Company found in Altoona.

"The Underwood Coal Company was purchased this year by parties affiliated with the Alabama Steel and Wire Company and it was certain to enter the main holdings. The property is twenty miles from Gadsden but was practically inaccessible for the lack of railroad transportation at that time. With the completion of the Altoona branch of the L&N railway the mines were placed in such proximity to Gadsden as to afford the Steel Company a 12.5 rate per ton on coal from Altoona. The mines are now, and have been for some time turning out a very fine quality of steam and cooking coal. The property covers 3,100 acres and there are holdings nearby that add to the total."

Mining in Altoona continued under Southern Steel Company

name. The mines expanded out of Blount County and into Etowah. Many mines owned by the Southern Steel Company were leased out to other operators. In 1913 another buyout occurred and Southern Steel Company became Gulf States Steel Co.

By 1913 the original "Underwood Drifts" were now known as Altoona No. 5 and were still being actively mined. It employed 185 miners who were paid 69¢, had a fan for ventilation and used Monobel as an explosive. The mine produced 120,000 tons of coal and was worked 275 days out of the year. The following description is given for Altoona Mine No 5: *"This is a drift opening on the Black Creek Seam, 2'10" high. Roof is slate and sand stone, the slate requiring careful timbering. Coal is gathered by mules and delivered to tipple. Mine is ventilated with a 6-foot Stine fan. Air is conducted through the mine on continuous current, using two splits. Coal is shot from solid with Monobel. Mine is naturally wet,"* Also operating as part Altoona No. 5 was Altoona D. It has the exactly same description except it was ventilated with a furnace instead of a fan. Forty of the 185 men were employed in this mine.

By 1916, 207 miners were employed and black powder was used.

In 1923 227 were employed, earned 94¢ a ton, and worked 307 days. In this report it is stated that coal is carried to the tipple by a steam dinky.

In 1926, 213 were employed, paid 80¢ per ton, and worked 284 days. This report states Gulf States Steel's mines as Altoona Drifts, and Vanzandt (Owned by Gulf States but leased.)

The final report comes from 1929. In this year 115,223 tons of coal were mined over 300 days. Pay remained at 80¢ a ton.

In 1932 Gulf States Steel closed its operation in Altoona. The property continued to be leased by the company (now named Republic Steel), until 1947 when they sold the property to Harry Brown. Note that Underwood/Southern Steel/Gulf State Steel has more mines than No. 5 (One example would be No. 17.) However it is the only mine that has been documented.

-Mining Methods-

This large-scale industrial mining differed greatly from the small "bootleg" mining that had existed years before. Once a vein was found a drift was made, supported by wooden timbers. It is all of this was done by hand with picks and shovels. It was a laborious job.

Mineshaft supported by timber

Next men would take a drill bit attached to a hand crank and drill a

hole into the coal vein to insert

Example of a drill bit

explosives.

The two types of explosive used were black powder and Monobel (a type of permissible.) Black powder was very cheap and accessible type of explosive. It was possible that black powder could ignite gases or coal dust in a mine making it a very dangerous explosive. Unfortunately it is a low explosive, which means that it lacks high pressure on explosion. This can be seen in how black powder propels a bullet but does not destroy the barrel. This makes it is less suitable compared to high explosives in mining.

A permissible explosive on the other hand is a very high explosive. It was specifically made for mining for the fact it wouldn't ignite gases or coal dust. Monobel was the permissible explosive used in the Altoona mines.

It was manufactured by the DuPont Company and was specifically designed for use in wet mines and blasting through hard rock and coal.

After detonation a narrow gauge railway known as "dinky gauge" was laid down inside the mine. Rail cars were brought in and loaded with coal. The cars were then pulled outside of the mine by mules.

As the mine expanded, a method called "room and pillar" mining was used. Think of city streets and blocks; the streets are where the coal is removed and the blocks are where coal is left to support the top.

This is essentially what room and pillar is. It is one of the oldest mining methods; on average it mines 60% of the coal although many factors could result in a higher percentage.

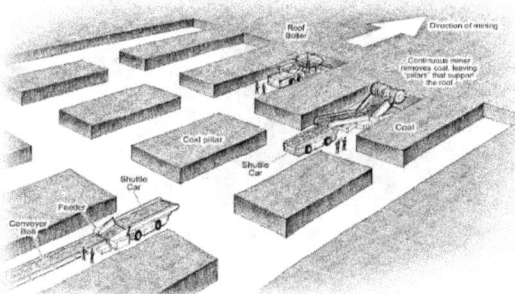
Example of room and pillar mining

When the mine expands and more rooms are opened ventilation becomes an important factor. Without proper ventilation miners could suffocate or gasses and dust could build up to fatal levels. The Altoona mines utilized three different methods of ventilation: natural, furnace, and fan. The figure below demonstrates a mine with all three ventilation methods represented by the letters A, and B.

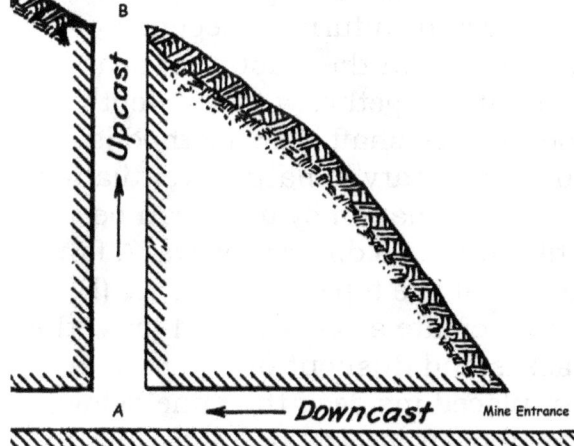

Natural ventilation is produced in a mine when there is a difference in elevation between the intake (mine entrance) and outlet airways (B) and a difference in temperature between the two openings. This would create a downcast and up cast, thus constantly flushing fresh air through the mine.

Example of Natural Ventilation at Altoona Mine No.5, December 2009.

Using a furnace is possible by placing the furnace at the bottom of the up cast (A). Furnaces are usually constructed of brick with air chambers on either side to prevent from heating the surrounding earth. The heated air passing over the furnace and entering the up cast is lighter than the cool air in the downcast shaft and is consequently forced upward. The quantity of air produced by a furnace depends principally on the amount of heat generated together with the depth of the furnace shaft. This method is complimentary to natural ventilation.

Ventilation by a fan can be utilized in two different ways. A fan placed at the top of the updraft (B) would create a vacuum and draw the gasses and dust out of the mine. A fan placed inside of the mine below the updraft (A) would pull fresh air into the mine. The mines in Altoona probably used method A. This was because of the design of the fan used, the Stine fan. S.B. Stine & Sons in Osceola, Pennsylvania manufactured it. The fan and motor in the picture below are shown mounted on a sub base. The fan had a 20-horsepower motor. It was controlled by a compound controller, which permitted the fan to run from minimum to maximum speed. The gearing between the motor and fan shafts had a ratio of 3 to 1. All of the bearings were lined with the best anti-friction metal and had the Stine improved ring-oiling device that only required oiling at intervals of about once a month. The motor was a four-pole slow-speed type, and all parts were standard which made repairs expedient. The fan motor and gearing were both enclosed making it both dust and waterproof. The 6-foot version of the fan which was the one found at the Altoona mines, was able to move 30,000 to 40,000 cubic feet of air per minute.

Illustration of a Stine Fan.

This fan ran continually on a split current. The split current allowed the fan to push air through the mine at a much more efficient rate.

Once the coal was outside of the mine it went to a coal washer. The coal washer was more or less like a modern washing machine. It combined water and vibration to remove impurities from the coal and the coal was then classified by the number of impurities remaining. At this time few regulations existed so most of these impurities known as "coal sludge" found their way into rivers and streams. According to a 1912 report the Southern Steel Company used a Stewart Coal Washer. The Stewart washer was very common at the time. It could treat 34 tons of raw coal in an hour in a pan that was 4½ft. by 7ft. in size. The pan made 37 strokes, 4in. in length per minute. First the coal was crushed. Then it was brought up a conveyor once at the top it dropped into a side and finally into the washer. From there it went up another elevator and into the settling tank. Then it was taken by the washed coal elevator and dumped into a tipple. Train cars would then back under the tipple and be filled with coal. The coal would then be carried to factories and industries by train. While the entire process was much more in depth these few pages should give a general description of the method used by the Underwood Coal Company and its descendants in mining coal from the Altoona mines. The hardest thing to grasp is the amount of labor used in mining at this time. It was dangerous, dirty, and hard work. While mechanical devices such as the Stewart coal washer made work easier and efficient. It is the men in the mines all day from sun up to sun down who still had to put forth the labor to power the homes, businesses, factories, and industries of the day.

Below is a list of superintendents and foremen for Gulf States Steel:

Year	Superintendent	Foreman
1913-1916	Frank House	L.T. Taylor
1920-1922	A.L. Rankin	
1922	Joseph Cain	B.K. Walker
1926-1927	Joseph Cain	O.D. Neighbors
1927-1929	Harry Brown	B.K. Walker

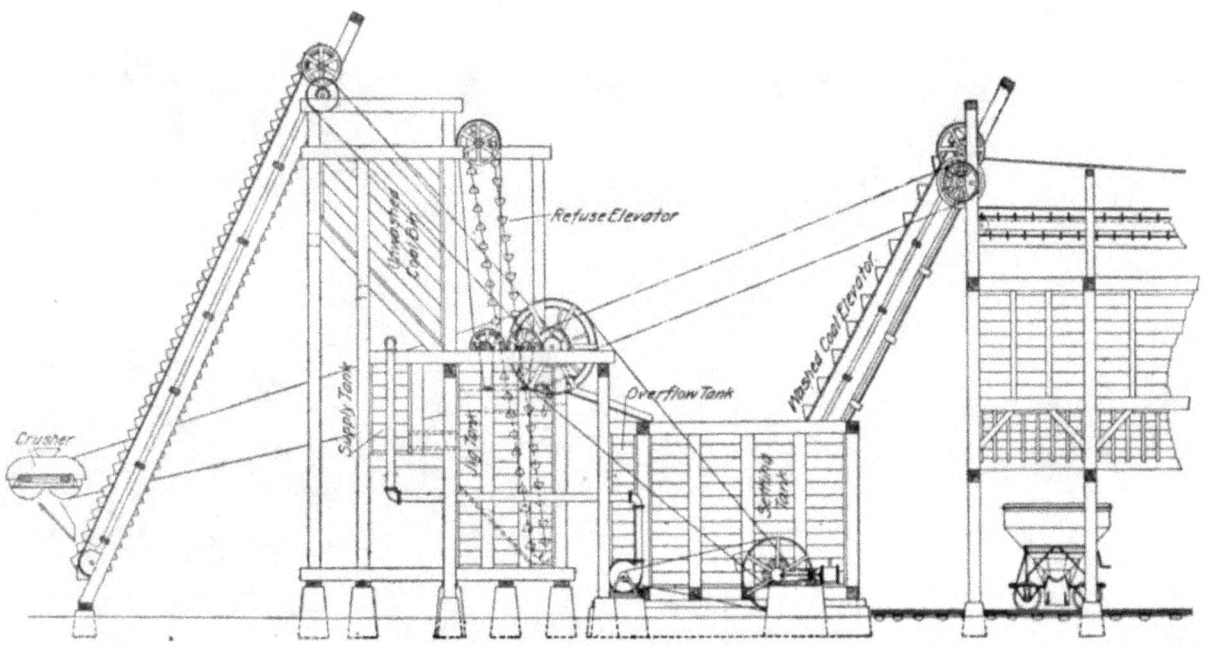

Stewart Coal Washer

Miners from the No. 17 coal mine in Altoona, around 1938 or 1939

Standing: Preacher Edwards, Harry White, Drexel Thompson, Floyd Jones, Pinkney Bramblett, Hewitt Self, Preacher Herd, Albert Arbor, Hubert Jones

Kneeling: Hoss Edwards, Edward Self, Lonnie Cheaves, Harry Warner, Grover Davenport, Herb Davenport, Amos Bragg.

Section of Underwood Drifts, Altoona No.5.

Mining Tools dug up on Altoona property. (Horseshoe, File, Punch, Bolt, Mule Shoe, and assorted spikes.) Special thanks to Mr. Gary Hilburn.

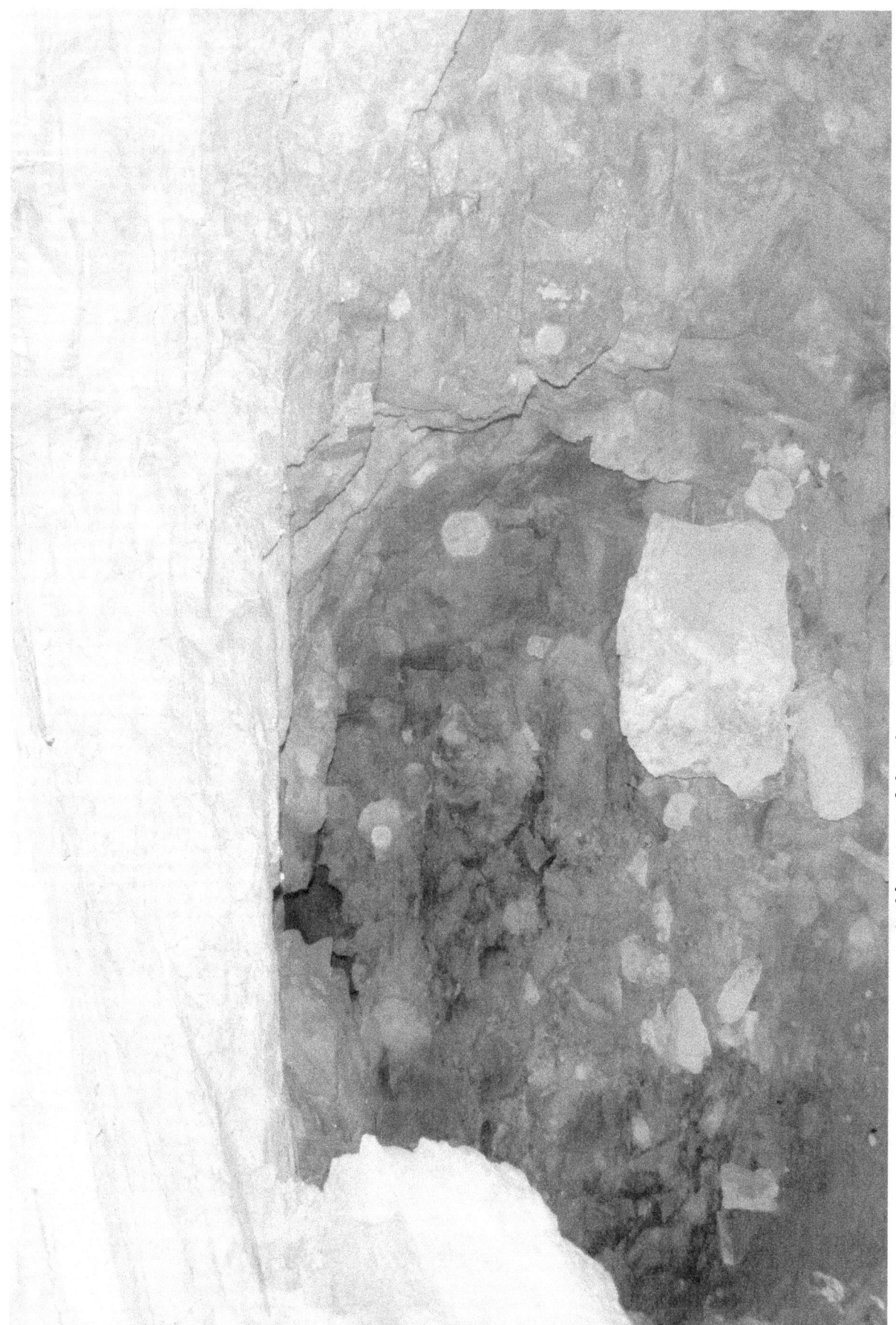

Inside a part of the Altoona No. 5 Mine, November 2009.

Boiler used as a culvert.

Dinky (mine car) track notched and bent. Special thanks to Gary Hilburn.

-Other Mining Operations-

The Underwood Coal Company was not the only company to try their luck at mining coal in Altoona. Many other individuals and companies mined the mountains.

In 1904 S.H. and T.P. Wood both had separate mining operations in Altoona nothing further is known of their operation, but it was probably comparable to the mining operations that existed before the Underwood Company. By 1906 the Wood's operation had ended.

Also in 1904 Geo. Vanzandt bought property east of Altoona on be back of the mountain. By 1905 he had purchased a section in Vanzandt Hollow from Underwood Coal Co. Mr. Vanzandt would retain this property until 1920. It seems that Mr. Vanzandt may have been associated with the Southern Steel Co. This fact is backed by the numerous "Southern" stamped bricks found on the site (such as the one seen a few pages back). We know from a lease record from Mr. Vanzandt to the Altoona Coal and Iron Co. in 1910 that it was a sizeable operation. The record states, *"All interested in a lease of coal lands located ½ mile from west Altoona, being known as the Vanzandt property together with all improvements thereon consisting of mine cars, rail, iron drums, wire ropes, tipple, pumps, blacksmith shop, and all other improvements thereon."*

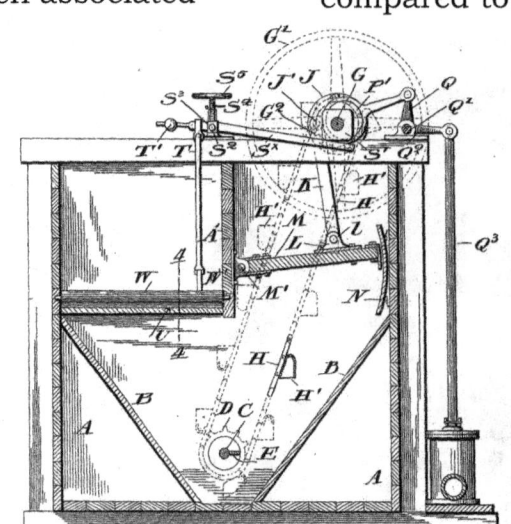

Montgomery Coal Washer

In 1907 the Blount Mountain Coal Co. started mining in Altoona. By 1910 they had dissolved. No further information is known.

On September 24, 1909, the Raccoon Mining Company was incorporated. It seems this company was also associated with the Southern Steel Company due to three of the four owners having a surname of Schuler. Schuler was also the surname of two of the owners of the Southern Steel Company. The Raccoon Mining Company leased property southwest of Altoona from both J.N. Rickles and the Southern Steel Co. They mined what was known as the Altoona No. 4 Mine. There is some information available about their operation and it seemed that it was a fairly sizeable operation. Although it was still small in size compared to Gulf States Steel.

In 1913 they operated the No. 4 as a drift mine and employed 126 men. Coal was picked manually and a total of 43 tons was mined during 1913. The miners were paid 52¢ a ton and they worked 291 days out of the year. A furnace was used as ventilation with both permissible and black powder as an explosive. The mine was described as having a roof of slate and sandstone requiring careful timbering. Coal was gathered by mules and delivered to an incline; from there it was lowered by gravity into the tipple and washed by a Montgomery Coal Washer, (only 200 tons a load). The mine was described as naturally wet. 1913 was also a year of lows for the company. Their $5,000 commissary located on what is now 7th avenue, across from the Altoona car wash was destroyed during the 1913 Altoona fire.

By 1916 only 93 men were employed with the Raccoon Mining Company.

In 1926 only 10 workers were employed at Altoona 4A. Raccoon Mining had also leased part of the Vanzandt property and had 16 miners employed there. Miners were paid $1.25 a ton and they worked 150 days out of the year. Black powder was used as an explosive and a furnace ventilated both mines. By 1929 the company had dissolved. The following men are listed as superintendent and mine foreman:

Year	Superintendent	Mine Foreman
1913	W.L. Smith	T.F. Winters
1916	R.V. Huff	R.V. Huff
1926	W.L. Smith	W.W. Smith
1926 Vanzandt Mine		W.D. Lee

On Nov. 7, 1910 the Altoona Coal and Iron Co. was organized. As previously stated they leased property from Mr. Vanzandt. It is unknown how long the company lasted but because lack of records and other leases it seems it dissolved sometime before 1922.

The Altoona Coal Co. was organized on May 26, 1917. Records show that they leased the Altoona No.4 property from Raccoon Mining Company. No other information is known. This company disbanded sometime before 1926. In 1923 H.L. Gruman was listed as mine foreman and J.O. Vernon as mine superintendent.

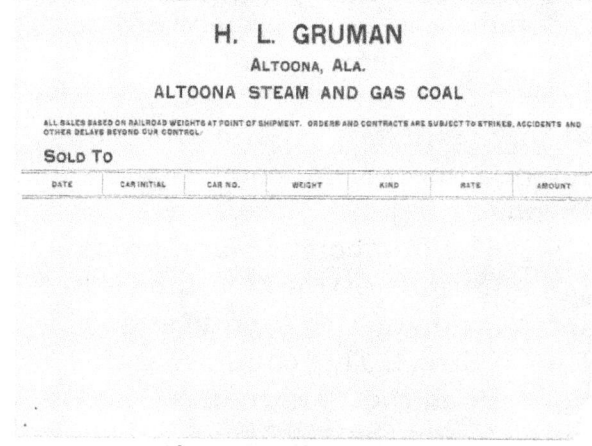

Altoona Coal Co. Invoice

Between 1916 and 1923. J.E. Bachus ran the Bachus Mine. J.C. Cooley was superintendent and mine foreman. The company disbanded before 1926. No further information is known.

On May 22, 1924, the Vanzandt Coal Co. was incorporated. They leased all of the property from Geo. Vanzandt. However Mr. Vanzandt was not associated with the company in any way. On February 6, 1925 Vanzandt Coal Co. filed a lawsuit for breach of contract against a land company. Not long after this the company disappears from the record.

A mine at Altoona No. 4 (circa 2010)

-The Commissary-

A commissary is a company store. Workers of the company have a special currency that they can spend at that store for food and provisions. Altoona had several commissaries through the years.

The first commissary, probably built around 1901 was located at the intersection of 10th Avenue and Brown Street. This commissary appears on the 1912 map of Altoona, and later on the 1923 map although it was not in use at that time. About 150 feet behind this commissary was the stable used for mules and horses used in the mining operation. Numerous horseshoes found in that area also confirm this fact.

In late 1912 or early 1913 another commissary was built. It was located at the corner of 4th Avenue, and Brown Street. That building stood until the late 1960's.

As stated earlier the Raccoon Mining Co. had a commissary on 7th Avenue, which burned down in 1913. It is unknown if they rebuilt in the same location.

Gulf State Steel Commissary in 1917. Photo taken by J.R. Bragg.

View from inside the commissary.

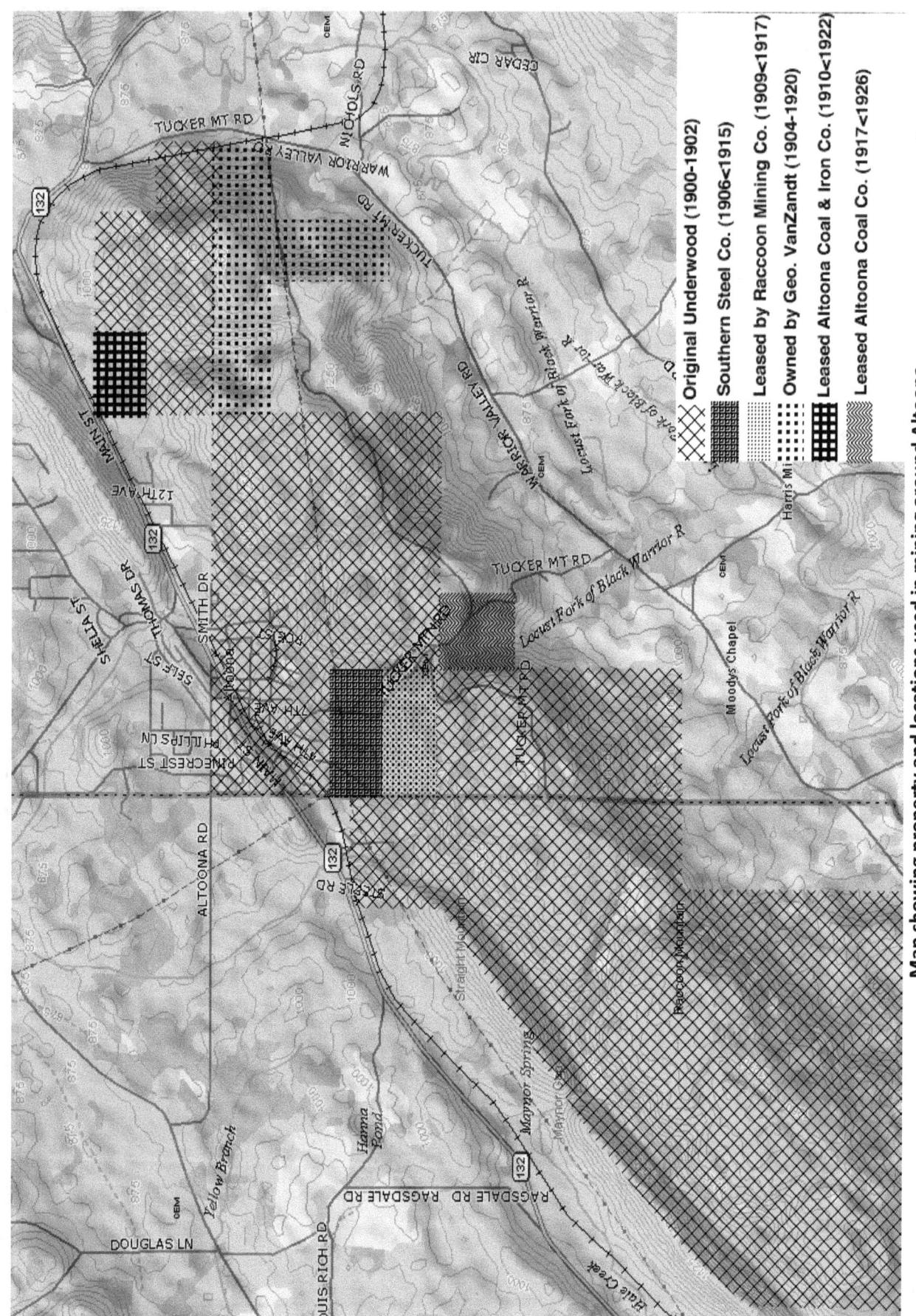

Map showing property and locations used in mining around Altoona.

-Later Mining Activity-

After Republic Steel ended operations in Altoona in 1932 the property they owned was leased out to other companies or individuals. Cherokee Mining Co., C.A. Tarpley, R.S. Blanton, Garvis Nichols and J.R. Sullivan (whose operation included a commissary) are several men who had leases on the property. This period marks a transition from in ground mining to surface or strip mining.

In the early 1940's Hugh Schuff started strip mining around Tait's Gap. Strip mining is the practice of mining a seam of coal by first removing a long strip of overlying soil and rock. Davis Robbins bought out Mr. Schuff and purchased the Republic Steel property in 1955. His strip mining yielded about 400 tons of coal a day. In the early 1960's Mr. Robbins built a shop and placed a tipple in Altoona near the depot. His mining operation continued until the early to mid-1970's. The property was then leased to the Basin Coal Company. This was the end of mining around Altoona, and by the mid 1980's all operations had ceased.

Davis Robbins and Hugh Schuff

Robbins Coal Co. tipple in Altoona.

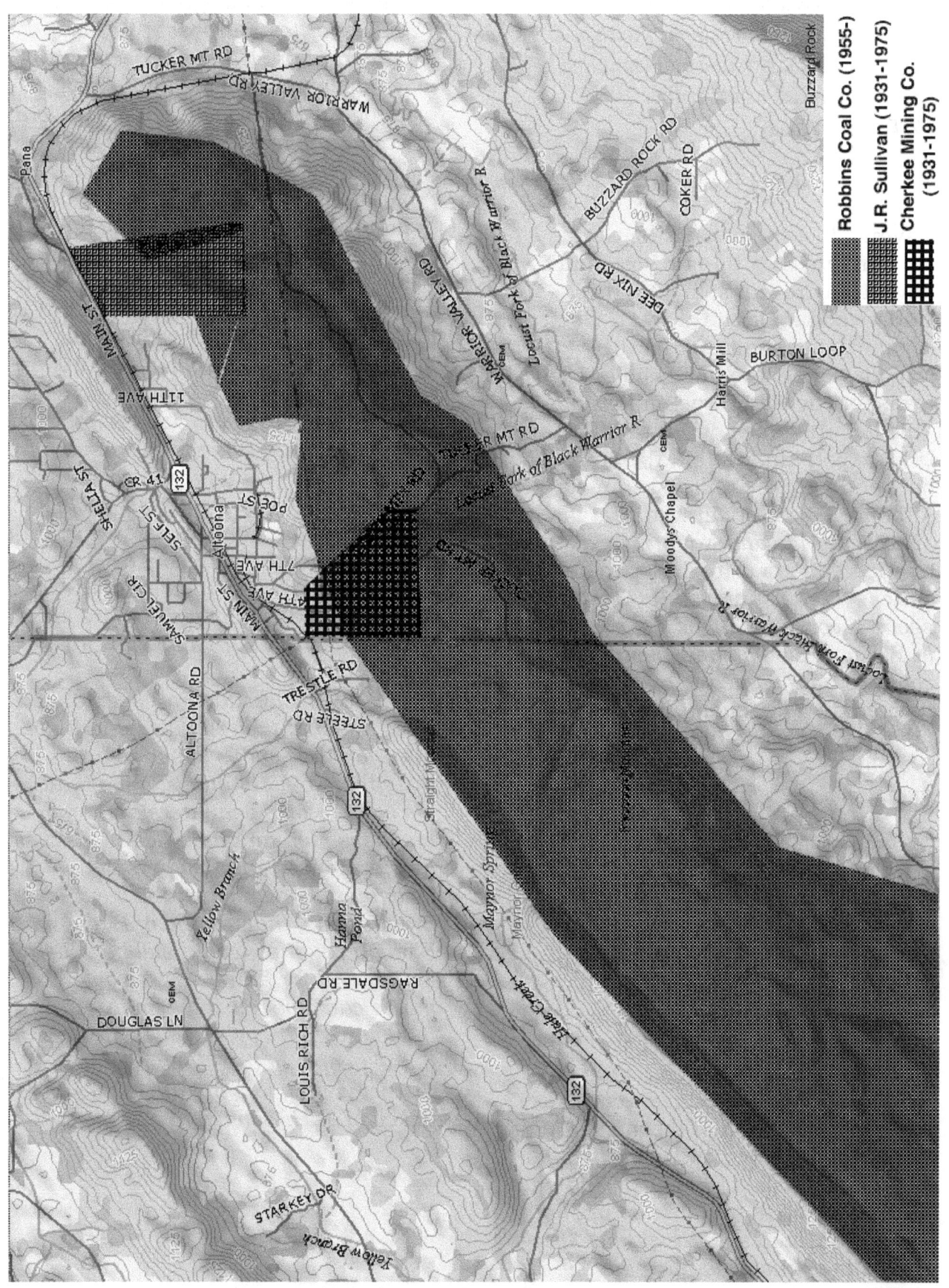

"Had it not been for Mr. Smith's desire to extend his railroad to help men with good propositions, that section of Blount and Etowah counties would still be asleep." – W.T. Underwood

-L&N Railroad-

Having all of the coal in the world wouldn't mean a thing if you didn't have a way to transport it. Mr. Underwood realized this fact. Due to the mines location transport by wagon was next to impossible; transport by water was impossible. This left only one option: rail. Mr. Underwood himself told the story of how and why the railroad came to Altoona. This story first appears in *"The Louisville and Nashville Railroad"* by Kincaid Herr. Mr. Underwood states, *"In the spring of 1900, I had secured control of a body of coal lands in Western Etowah and Blount counties and wanted to open mines. I wanted it badly, but my lands were many miles from a railroad, and I was not able to command one-third of the money needed. I preferred opening mines on that side of my property nearest to the Alabama Great Southern Railroad and took the matter up with the Southern officials, but got no encouragement. I then went to Mr. Milton H. Smith and found no difficulty in arousing his interest it. I remember his saying to me: 'If you have the quality and quantity of coal you think you have, I will build you a road.' I then explained that I could not raise more than one-third of the money needed for opening and operating the mines and I asked him if he could aid me with that. He said that he did not know but would see. He did not keep me waiting, but acted immediately. He made me haul 30 wagonloads of coal 12 miles for test purposes. He sent experts and proved the correctness of my statement as to quantity. He then arranged with a Louisville bank to loan my company many thousands of dollars, which we were allowed to payoff from our earnings. He began building 12 miles of road for us in May 1900, and the following October we were shipping coal over it. I started this business with but a few thousand dollars of my own and within four years' time had paid about $80,000 for the land, paid off the banks, and sold the property for a very large sum, most of which money came from outside of the State and remains invested in Alabama. The country through which he built the road and its extension on to Attalla, had been almost a wilderness. The population there has now increased ten times or more (this was written in 1910) and that city is prosperous.*

Other railroads had been asked to do this, but they did not. Had it not been for Mr. Smith's desire to extend the sphere of usefulness of his road, his comprehensive understanding of business men and their needs, as well as of railroads, and his personal inclination to help men with good propositions, that section of Blount and Etowah counties would still be asleep. Today and for fifty years to come, its mines can give a living to many thousands of people . . . The prosperity of the people of the Alabama mineral district is very largely due to the liberal policy of M.H. Smith."

The railroad first reached Altoona on January 1, 1901. At this time construction was halted until work resumed in May 1903 on the last 13.83-mile line linking Altoona to Attalla. This stretch took two years to complete due to the 2300 foot tunnel in Tumlin Gap. Construction of the tunnel was slow and many men lost their lives due to falling rocks or powder explosions. The first train ran from Altoona to Attalla on May 7, 1905. Passenger trains ran from its opening until the 1970's. Freight ran on the track until the late 1990's when the track was removed and the property was returned to the landowners.

-Culverts-

One of the interesting things about the railroad through Altoona is the culverts. Modern culverts a made out of concrete, corrugated plastic or steel pipe. The culverts used during the construction in 1900 are marvels of engineering. Hand hewn rock was stacked and mortared in place to create a culvert. All of the culverts in Altoona originated from a quarry at the Altoona No. 5 mine. One of the unfinished rocks can still be seen ready to be loaded and used.

Original stone culvert

Rock at Altoona No.5 ready for use as culvert, December 2009.

Passenger Timetables

1902 — Altoona and Birmingham

No. 45 EX SUN	Distance	Trains do not stop at Stations where no time is shown.	No. 44 EX SUN
6 00 AM	.0	Lv. Altoona Ar.	7 00 PM
6 35 AM	9.6	Champion	6 04 PM
7 00 AM	11.6	Oneonta	5 45 PM
7 13 AM	14.6	Chepultepec	5 32 PM
7 34 AM	19.8	Swansea	5 10 PM
7 50 AM	23.4	Remlap	4 55 PM
8 09 AM	27.2	Village Springs	4 39 PM
8 58 AM	36.8	Greens	3 58 PM
9 30 AM	44.9	Boyles	3 28 PM
9 55 AM	48.6	Ar. Birmingham Lv.	2 55 PM

1913 — Louisville & Nashville, Table No. 21, Birmingham, Anniston and Calera

81 DAILY	83 DAILY	85 DAILY	Distance	Trains do not stop at Stations where no time is shown.	86 DAILY	84 DAILY
PM	PM	AM			PM	AM
	3 40	8 35	.0	Lv. Birmingham Ar.	6 50	10 40
	3 49	8 45	3.0	Boyles	6 41	10 29
	f 4 01	8 56	6.8	Ketona	f 6 29	f 10 18
	f 4 11	9 06	11.0	Green's	f 6 19	f 10 09
	4 18	9 13	14.4	Mt. Pinson	6 12	10 02
	4 27	9 22	18.2	Palmers	6 04	9 55
	4 36	9 32	20.7	Village Springs	5 56	9 49
	4 44	9 41	24.6	Remlap	f 5 48	f 9 41
	4 52	9 50	25.3	Inland	5 40	9 33
	5 03	10 02	33.4	Chepultepec	5 28	9 22
	f 5 07	f 10 05	34.7	Mattawana	f 5 24	f 9 18
	5 11	10 10	36.5	Oneonta	5 21	9 14
	5 18	10 16	38.6	Champion	f 5 16	f 9 08
	5 34	10 34	47.7	Altoona	4 56	8 50
	5 45	10 46	52.5	Tumlin Gap	f 4 39	f 8 36
	5 57	10 59	60.6	Ivalee	f 4 24	f 8 21
	6 03	11 05	63.3	Moragne	f 4 18	f 8 17
	6 08	11 10	64.8	Attalla	4 12	8 12
	6 16	11 22	67.6	Alabama City	4 04	8 05
	6 22	11 33	70.1	Gadsden	3 53	7 54
	f 6 38	f 11 50	76.0	Glencoe	f 3 41	f 7 43
	6 43	11 57	78.1	Rock Springs	3 35	7 36
	f 6 52	f 12 07	82.5	Reads Mill	f 3 23	f 7 27
	f 6 57	f 12 12	84.2	Duke	f 3 19	f 7 23
	7 02	12 18	86.3	Wellington	3 13	7 16
	7 10	12 28	89.8	Alexandria	f 3 05	f 7 09
	7 21	12 40	94.5	Leatherwood	f 2 54	f 6 59
AM	7 35	12 55	99.3	Ar. Anniston Lv.	2 40	6 45
6 10	PM	1 15	99.3	Lv. Anniston Ar.	2 20	AM
6 31		f 1 34	107.9	Coldwater	2 00	
f 6 43		f 1 49	113.8	Munford	f 1 48	
6 59		2 04	120.8	Ironaton	1 32	
7 08		2 14	124.2	Stockdale	1 23	
7 20		2 25	129.2	Talladega	1 10	
f 7 40		f 2 46	138.8	Rendalra	f 12 49	
7 50		2 57	144.3	Sycamoe	12 38	
f 7 53		f 3 00	146.3	Enaubee	f 12 35	
8 04		3 13	151.5	Sylacauga	12 22	
f 8 12		f 3 20	154.2	Gantts Junction	f 12 17	
8 25		3 33	160.8	Fayetteville	12 05	
8 31		3 38	163.7	Talladega Springs	12 01	
f 8 42		f 3 49	168.2	Mosteller	f 11 50	
8 54		4 01	172.7	Shelby	11 40	
f 9 05		f 4 12	179.1	Springs Junction	f 11 28	
9 20		4 25	184.3	Ar. Calera Lv.	11 15	
AM		PM			AM	

1929 — Table 15, Birmingham, Anniston and Calera

44-83 Daily	46-85 Daily	Distance		47-86 Daily	45-84 Daily	
PM	AM			PM	AM	
5 00	8 25	.0	Lv. Birmingham, Ala. Ar.	6 20	9 55	a Nos. 83 and 84 stop on signal to pick up or let off passengers to or from Birmingham.
	8 35	3.0	" Boyles Ar	6 10		
	f 8 46	5.9	" Ketona "	f 6 01		f Train stops on signal.
	8 52	10.1	" Greens "	f 5 55		
f 5 26	8 59	13.6	" Mt. Pinson "	f 5 49	f 9 28	Nos. 81, 82, 85 and 86 stop on signal at G. P. Junction Okomo and Gascot.
	f 9 07	17.3	" Palmers "	f 5 43		
	9 18	19.8	" Village Springs "	5 35		
	f 9 25	23.7	" Remlap "	f 5 27		Nos. 85 and 86 stop on signal at Glencoe.
	9 32	27.4	" Inland "	5 21		
	9 40	32.5	" Chepultepec "	5 11		
	f 9 42	33.9	" Mattawana "	f 5 09		
5 58	9 48	35.6	" Oneonta "	5 03	8 54	
	f 9 55	37.2	" Champion "	f 4 58		
	10 00	41.2	" Taits Gap "	4 50		
6 16	10 11	46.7	" Altoona "	4 39	8 36	
f 6 26	f 10 22	52.5	" Tumlin Gap "	f 4 27	f 8 26	
	f 10 35	59.5	" Ivalee "	f 4 13		
	f 10 39	62.3	" Moragne "	f 4 09		
6 45	10 43	63.7	" Attalla "	4 01	8 06	
f 6 53	10 55	66.5	" Alabama City "	3 55	f 8 01	
7 00	11 03	68.5	" Gadsden "	3 45	7 55	
	f		" Fourth and Locust Sts. "	f	f	
	f 11 31	81.4	" Read's Mill "	f 3 14		
	f 11 35	83.2	" Duke "	f 3 10		
	11 39	85.3	" Wellington "	3 05	f 7 27	
f 7 28	f 11 47	88.8	" Alexandria "	f 2 58	a	82 Daily
	f 11 55	93.6	Lv. Leatherwood "	f 2 50		PM
	12 15	98.4	Ar. Anniston Lv.	2 35	f 8 01	7 40
81 Daily	12 40	98.4	Lv. Anniston Ar.	2 20	AM	7 25
AM	f 12 55	106 5	" Coldwater Lv.	f 2 05		f 7 13
6 05	1 07	112.4	" Munford "	1 52		f 7 08
f 6 20	f 1 14	115.6	" McElderry "	f 1 45		f 7 06
6 32	1 21	120.0	" Ironaton "	f 1 37		f 6 55
f 6 39	f 1 29	123.3	" Stockdale "	f 1 29		f 6 50
6 46	1 41	128.4	" Talladega "	1 15		6 37
6 53	f 1 58	137.5	" Rendalia "	f 12 58		f 6 20
7 03	2 08	143.4	" Sycamore "	12 48		6 10
7 22	2 21	149.8	" Sylacauga "	12 32		5 55
7 31	2 30	152.6	" Gantts Junction "	12 27		5 50
7 44	f 2 40	159.3	" Fayetteville "	12 14		f 5 38
7 54	2 46	162.1	" Talladega Springs "	12 08		5 33
8 04	f 2 56	166.5	" Mosteller "	f 11 58		f 5 23
8 10	3 08	171.9	" Shelby "	11 46		5 11
8 20	f 3 18	177.5	Lv. Springs Junction "	f 11 36		f 5 01
8 43	3 30	182.7	Ar. Calera, Ala. Lv.	11 25		4 50
8 55	AM			AM		PM

-Altoona Depot-

During these early years the unofficial life center of the town was the depot. All shipments and mail made to and from Altoona depended on it. The first depot was built in 1901. It was a simple building next to the tracks. The exact location of this depot is unknown; however in a 1903 property deed map Mr. Underwood lists the "Depot Lot" close to the intersection of 10th Avenue and Brown Street. Whether this was the location of the depot or a planned site is unknown.

By 1905, a newer depot was located between Robbins Road and St. Clair Street. Then around 1909 or 1910 the L&N Railroad built a new $5,000 depot at the same location. This is the depot that stood until the early 1970's.

Below is a list of men that worked at the Altoona depot as agents:

Opening-1902	Henry Meacham
1907	W.E. Brown
1911	John Kaufman
1920-1924	O.B. Powell
1937	Mrs. Bertie P. Moore
1947	R.E. Vernon
1957	O.B. Powell
From 1957 on Altoona utilized Oneonta's agent	
1960	A.J. Dover
1968	D. McGrady
1971	W.J. Smith

Location Of "Depot Lot" On Mr. Underwood's 1903 deed.

Original Depot. Pictured L to R: David H. Crump, Miss Nan Lee, Mr. McIntire, Miss Jennie Crump, John Cole, Miss Annie Cole, Henry Meacham, and Miss Cornelius. Photo taken in May 1902.

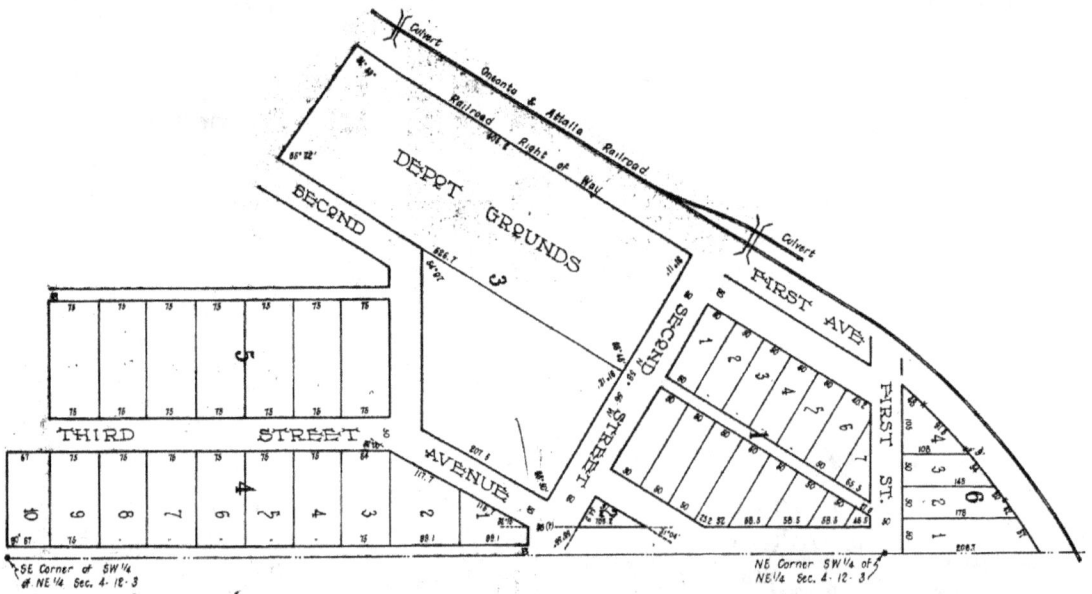

1905 plat showing the location of the depot between Robbins Road and St. Clair Street.

Picture of depot shortly after its construction, about 1909 or 1910.

"No more gracious hospitality can be found in Etowah County than in Altoona. The delicious meals in their homes cannot be surpassed." – Denson Franklin

-The Name-

The name Altoona first appears in a Blount County News Dispatch article on October 11, 1900. The article entitled "A New Town" states that *"Altoona is the name given to W.T. Underwood's new mines in Blount County."* Where did this name come from? There are two theories.

The first theory states that experienced miners from Altoona Pennsylvania came down to work in the mines and thus brought the names with them. Examination of the census at the time shows that not one of Altoona's residents came from Pennsylvania. The closest resident to Pennsylvania was born in Illinois. One could also argue that Altoona Pennsylvania was well known at the time for its industrial heritage. That is true but Altoona was a center for railroading, not coal mining.

The other theory focuses on the etymology of the word Altoona. Upon examination the word is derived from the German word of Altona, which means "all to near." However, there is another language that you can derive Altoona from. That language is Cherokee. Within it is the word Allatoona, which means "high lands of great worth." This fits as a perfect description for the area in the early 1900's. Unfortunately it is unknown how the town really came upon the name.

-Building a Town-

Some of the earliest abstracts we have of Altoona come from newspapers at the time. Little is known of Altoona between its founding and 1902 but it grew very fast in a short amount of time. The first real story comes from a picnic at Altoona on July 5, 1902. A writer from the Southern Democrat in a July 10 article entitled "The Picnic At Altoona" wrote: *A large crowd of probably 2000 people assembled on the picnic grounds,* (where the tennis courts and recreational center are today) *by 11 o'clock in the morning. Farmers, Merchants, Miners, Preachers, Doctors, Railroad Men, all classes came to golden and enjoy the occasion.*

Mr. W.T. Underwood, president of the Underwood Coal Company extended to the people a warm and cordial welcome that made each and every one feel at home. All were impressed with the sincerity, earnestness, and good taste of the hearty greeting.

Dr. J.A. Hurst of Walnut Grove responded to the welcome with a brief address expressing appreciation to the Underwood Coal Co. and the people of Altoona, who was the host of the celebration. Making all preparation and arrangements necessary to the comfort of the people. Dr. Hurst touched incidentally on the great problems of the hour in a thoughtful vein of encouragement.

Mr. Hubert T. Davis, of Gadsden came to represent Col. W.T. Dortch of Gadsden who was on the program for

a speech on "Our industrial condition and prospects." Mr. Davis made a strong speech on our industrial possibilities and an eloquent plea for the cultivation of friendly relations between capital and labor.
Walnut Grove Lodge No. 264 A.F. and A.M. held a public installation of officers.

Dinner was announced and the baskets of the people were opened revealing the abundance of wholesome material for the refreshment of the inner man.

At 2 P.M. the people were called together and addressed by several gentlemen on the various phases of the odd fellowship.

Judge T.H. Davidson of Oneonta dwelt on the history and mission of the order, showing the true basis of human happiness to rest on the profession of a sound principles and faithful performance of duty.

Rev. W.J. Nash of Walnut Grove emphasized the duty of a man to man, and man's duty to God as inoculated by the order, and revealed in the parable of the good Samaritan.

Henry Page Burruss of Altoona, Ala. showed the close kinship and striking harmony and congeniality existing between the free institutions of the American Republic and principles of the I.O.O.F. thus accounting for the wonderful growth of the order in America and the country of Tentonic Blood.

Music for the occasion was furnished by Mrs. Frank Fowler and Miss Gertrude Roberts of Oneonta Ala., and Mrs. H.P. Burruss and daughter Miss Elsie. And Louise Roberts of Altoona, Ala. Mr. J.B. Cleveland was active and zealous in the direction of the musical program.

Mr. D.H. Crump supervisor of the picnic grounds deserves the highest commendation for his energetic attention to the many details involving the welfare and comfort of the people on this occasion. Capt. A.J. Phillips Noble Grand of the Etowah Lodge No. 97 I.O.O.F. presided with dignity and grace ably assisted in the direction of the program by Mr. B.W. Reavis the Secretary of the lodge who is always at the post of duty and efficient and attentive at every point of duty.

Mess. F. Culverhouse, J.H. Taylor, W.W. Sullivan, T.E. Harris and D.L. Sullivan committee on reception and order were active, alert, efficient and attentive at every point of duty.

The good order, good humor and courteous conduct of the vast throng of people on this occasion was a tribute to the good me of Altoona and the entire character of the people of Etowah and Blount.

The program was opened with prayer and close with the benediction by Rev. J.S. DeLache of Oneonta.

Many were the expressions, on the part of the visitors of surprise, pleasure and admonition at the development and growth that have taken place at Altoona within the last two years.

The next article on Altoona comes from the *Attalla Mirror* on July 5, 1904. It states, "Altoona is one of Etowah County's hustling little towns. It is a mining town, but the population is a good class of people and seldom any trouble is heard of there. A number of stores are now open, a large company commissary and various other enterprises. In fact, Altoona is a little city and her population is growing daily."

Other articles speak of the school and churches present in the town at the time and how it continued to grow. An April 7, 1905 article from the *Attalla Mirror* talks of the Southern Bell Telephone Company running a line from Attalla to Altoona for telephone service.

The following are business listings by year for Altoona up to 1908:

1901: Hamilton and Starkey (General Store)
M.F. Walker and Sons (General Store)
1903: P.D. Holland (General Store)
W.D. Debtor (General Store)
W.T. Smith and Company (General Store)
R.D. Stanfield (Grocer)
H.L. Starkey (General Store)
M.F. Walker and Co. (General Store)
Watson and Nash (Meats)
1904: P.D. Bullard (General Store)
W.J. Cleveland and Co. (General Store)
W.D. Debtor (General Store)
W.H. Jackson (General Store)
W.T. Smith and Company (General Store)
R.D. Stanfield (Grocer)
H.L. Starkey (General Store)
M.F. Walker and Co. (General Store)
Watson and Nash (Meats)
S.H. Wood (General Store and Mining)
T.F. Wood (Coal Miner)
1905: Sam Baker (Dry Goods)
F.M. Bates (Grocer)
M.W. Brice (General Store)
P.D. Bullard (General Store)
W.J. Cleveland and Co. (General Store)
G.A. Cole (General Store)
J.J. Cook (Grocer)
D.H. Crump (Grocer)
Dupree Furniture Co.
H.B. Gary (Grocer)
M.E. Guinead and Son (Grocer)
J.T. Reese (Grocer)
C.S. Sherrell (Grocer)
Robert Stanfield (Grocer)
H.L. Starkey (General Store)
G.S. Stephens (General Store)
S.L. Stubbs (Drugs)
Thompson and Thompson (General Store)
Walker and Sons (General Store)
S.H. Wood (General Store and Mining)
T.F. Wood (Coal Miner)
1906: Sam Baker (Dry Goods)
J.T. Blalock (General Store)
W.J. Cleveland and Co. (General Store)
D.H. Crump (Grocer)
Dooley and Brown (Sawmill)
Dupree Furniture Co.
Ellison Bros (Drugs)
B.F. Guinead (Grocer)
I.H. Horton (General Store)
Charles Miller (General Store)
S.F. Oliver (General Store)
L.L. Owen (General Store)
B. Rosenbloom (Dry Goods)
Robert Stanfield (Grocer)
H.L. Starkey (General Store)
G.S. Stephens (General Store)
A.A. Stewart (General Store)
Osgood Taylor (Dry Goods)
J.F. Thompson (General Store)
Walker and Hullet (General Store)
W.D. White (General Store)
1907: Sam Baker (Dry Goods)
J.T. Blalock (General Store)
Blount Mountain Coal Co.
W.J. Cleveland and Co. (General Store)
G.A. Cole (General Store)
Dooley and Brown (Sawmill)
Dupree Furniture Co.
Ellison Bros (Drugs)
B.F. Guinead (Grocer)
I.H. Horton (General Store)
W.O. Hullet (General Store)

C.A. Johnston (Photography)
R.L. McEntire (General Store)
H.L. McGill (General Store and Mill)
Charles Miller (General Store)
Philips and Arnold (General Store)
H.W. Pickens (Meats)
Mrs. E.R. Pratt (Milly)
B. Rosenbloom (Dry Goods)
Robert Stanfield (Grocer)
H.L. Starkey (General Store)
A.A. Stewart (General Store)
Osgood Taylor (Dry Goods)
J.F. Thompson (General Store)
J.C. Waid and Sons (General Store)
Walker and son (General Store)
M.F. West (Cold Drinks)
W.D. White (General Store)

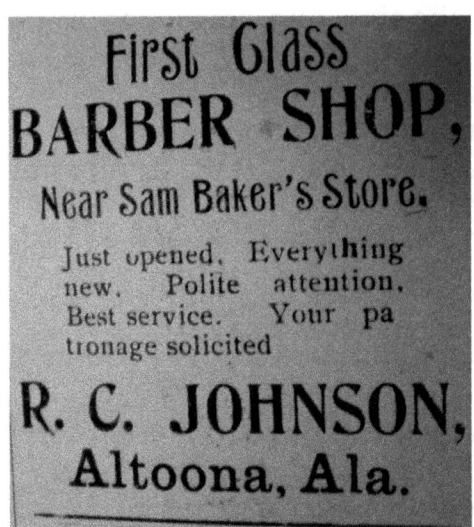

Business Advertisement, circa 1908.

Business was booming, but some sort of government was needed. That would finally happen in 1908.

Lucille White and brothers in front of W.D. White's general store.

-Governing Altoona-

Like every growing town Altoona felt a need for some sort of government. It is not known exactly when, but early on Altoona had a government by constabulary.

A constable is someone who is elected in each precinct. Constables have full powers of arrest, stop, and search within their precinct. They are generally responsible for serving warrants as well as patrolling the streets and providing security for civic events. They are not funded from general tax revenues; instead, they are paid by the number of criminals they arrest. In 1906 and 1907, W.M. Lee was constable for Altoona.

Even under this system the people exercised great power. In mid-1907 they gathered enough supporters to call for a vote on prohibition. On October 31, 1907, the *Attalla Mirror* reported, *"The polls have just closed and the vote stands at 28 to 1 in favor of prohibition. The day has been an ideal one and everything went off quiet. At 11 o'clock the school and ladies marched through the town singing, 'We're battling it right.' It was a sight never to be forgotten."*

Unfortunately by government under constabulary Altoona was not an incorporated municipality. They could not tax nor could they provide for public works. In 1905 the citizens of the town made four attempts to incorporate as a town. All four were declared void. By August of 1905 on the fifth attempt Judge Penn declared the petition was right with the proper number of signatures and gave the boundary limits and all other information by law. However something was wrong with the conduct of the election and as a result it was declared illegal. On November 12, 1907 the sixth petition was filed with probate judge J.W. Penn. The petition states:

"The State Of Alabama Probate Court Etowah County Nov. 12, 1907 Before the honorable J.W. Penn judge of probate for said county.
Be it remembered that on this day of November 1907 the following petition was filed with the honorable J.W. Penn Judge of probate for said county. The undersigned respectfully represent unto your honor that they are inhabitants of the territory embraced within the following boundaries.

Beginning at the north west corner of the south west quarter of the south east quarter of section thirty-three, township eleven range, three east. Then east 3960 feet to the north east corner of the south west quarter of section thirty-three, township eleven range, three east. Thence north 58 degrees east 2590 feet to a stake on straight mountain. Thence east along the land line 412 feet to the north east corner of the north west quarter of the south east quarter of section thirty-three, township eleven range, three east. Thence south 18 degrees east 2816 feet to a stake on the township line between townships 11 & 12 range 3 east. Thence south 39 degrees west 3815 feet to a stake. Thence west 1200 to a stake. Thence south 48 degrees west 3200 feet to the south east corner of the south west quarter of the southeast quarter of section four, township 12, range 3 east. Thence west along the section line 1320 feet to the south west corner of the south east quarter of said section four. Thence north along the line between the counties of Etowah and Blount one and one fourth miles to the beginning point in Etowah County, Ala. The afore described territory is now an unincorporated community that the undersigned are inhabitants thereof are desirous of incorporating the same into a municipality under the name of Altoona. That population of the same is less than one hundred nor more than three thousand and that the said undersigned further represents that in addition to being inhabitants and residence of said territory they are qualified electors and free holders therein. Therefore they would petition your honor to order an election to be held within the limits of the above described territory of a time and place to be designated by your honor and as provided by law for the purpose of the qualified electors residing in said territory voting upon the question as to whether or not the same shall be incorporated into a municipality as herein prayed.

The undersigned wound suggest that said election be held at W.J. Cleveland store house in Altoona and on _____ of _____ 1907. Attached to this petition an accurate plat of the territory embraced within the limits of the proposed municipality"

The petition was approved and a vote to incorporate took place on December 2, 1907 by a vote of 27–0. On December 13, 1907, Judge Penn appointed D.H. Crump, B.H. Ellison, and Daniel Hunt as commissioners to take a census of Altoona. This was needed for Altoona to be classified as either a town or city. On December 30, 1907, Judge J.W. Penn upheld the vote and Altoona became a municipal corporation.

On February 10, 1908, Altoona held its first municipal election. The vote was as follows:

For mayor: W.O. Hullett (4), T.W. Hood (12), W.M. Lee (1), C.L. Thompson (32).

For alderman: T.J. Bradshaw (18), I.S. Cook (2), B.H. Ellison (38), W.J. Ellison (18), S.S. Guinead (23), O.S. Goforth (13), John Goodwin (16), S.A. Hopper (17), A. McElham (5), B.N. Reavis (15), J.W. Reid (19), J.N. Rickles (2), J.C. Reid (5), W.C. Thompson (21), J.C. Waid (25).

Mr. C.L. Thompson was a real estate dealer, a business owner, and a prominent republican.

On February 18, 1908, Mr. Thompson was sworn in as mayor of Altoona before Judge J.W. Penn. Mayor Thompson called the first meeting that night. The following are the notes from that meeting:

The Board of Alderman called together by Mayor C.L. Thompson for the purpose of swearing in the officers and to transact such business as may be brought before the order.

Alderman elected: *B. H. Ellison, JC Waid, W.C. Thompson, S.S. Guinead and J.W. Reid was duly sworn in by mayor C.L. Thompson.*

The nomination of officers was declared in order.

For treasurer: *Dr. J.H. Ellison, W.D. White, W.O. Hullet*

Dr. J.H. Ellison was duly elected to the office of treasurer by Ellison, Waid and Thompson.
W.D. White secured two ballots by Guinead and Reid.

For clerk: *J.W. Waid Jr. and A.M. Phillips. A.M. Philips was duly elected by Reid, Ellison, and Thompson. J.C. Waid, Jr. Received two votes by Guinead and Waid.*

OATH OF OFFICE.

I, ~~J. C. Waid~~ The, do solemnly swear that I will support the constitution and laws of the UNITED STATES, and the constitution and law of the STATE of ALABAMA, so long as I continue A citizen thereof, and that I will honestly and faithfully discharge the duties of the office Upon which I am about to enter to the best of my ability, so help me GOD. sworn to and subscribed Before me this ~~February 15 1908~~ The 5 day of Oct, 1908.

C L Thompson   Mayor.

J.C. Waid Jr
J.W. Hood
J.F. Thompson
M. Vandiver
S.S. Guined
W.D. Pope
James Kay

DUELING OATH.

I, ~~J. C. Waid~~ The, Do solemnly swear that I have not directly, given, accepted or knowingly carried A Challenge, in writing or otherwise to any Person being A citizen of this state, to fight with deadly weapons either in or out of this state, or aided or abetted in the same since I have Been A citizen thereof: and that I will not directly or indirectly, give or accept, or knowingly carry A Challenge to any person, being A Citizen of this state, to fight with deadly weapons, either in or out of the state, or in any Manner aid or abet the same during my continuance in OFFICE. Sworn to and subscribed Before me. ~~this 15 Feb 1908~~ Oct 5 1908.

C L Thompson   Mayor.

M. Vandiver
J.W. Hood
J.F. Thompson
J.C. Waid Jr
S.S. Guined
W.D. Pope
James Kay

Original 1908 oath of office and dueling oath.

For chief of police: W.J. Cleveland, S.T. Green & J.C. Reid. J.C. Reid received one vote by Guinead. S.T. Green no votes, W.J. Cleveland four votes by Waid, Ellison, Thompson, and Reid.
W.J. Cleveland was duly elected chief of police.
For street overseer: V.B. Dunn & J.C. Waid Jr.

J.C. Waid Jr. was unanimously elected street overseer
Health officer: Dr. J.H. Ellison was approved.

Two days later the council met and passed the first two ordinances:
Ordinance #1: To fix the salary of the health officer of Altoona, Alabama for the year 1908. The compensation of the health officer shall be $1.00 per month.
Ordinance #2: To fix the salary of street overseer. Be it ordained by the mayor and board of aldermen of the town of Altoona and Alabama that this compensation to the street overseer shall be a $1.25 per day for each days service on the streets. Be it further ordained street overseer shall work 8 hours each day beginning at 8:00 AM and ending at 5:00 PM.
Be it further ordained that the street overseer shall not receive any compensation for warming hands.

Ordinances continued to be passed and elections were held. In 1913 after the fire in Altoona the council debated a public water system but the measure did not pass. On June 22, 1917 the Alabama Supreme Court declared that the incorporation of the town was illegal because the description of the original 1907 area was indefinite. *The Gadsden Times* article from June 22, 1917, reads: *"The case of the state of Alabama ex rel. T.D. Wagnon vs. the town of Altoona was reversed and remanded. The purpose of the proceedings was to dissolve the corporation of Altoona and to oust the mayor and aldermen. The case was appealed from the Etowah circuit court. As a result of this decision a highly prosperous mining town of 2,000 inhabitants is without a separate municipal government and the mayor, aldermen, and policemen are out of a job. Steps will be taken immediately to incorporate the town in a legal way and petitions to that end are being prepared. The proceedings were of a friendly nature and were brought by Culli & Martin as attorneys for Mr. Wagnon. White & Lusk represented the city of Altoona. The quo warrantee was filed before Judge A.O. Steele here a week ago. He denied the petition without going into it fully and it was hurried to the supreme court, which reached a decision in less than a week. Some time ago it was found that the map of the proposed town, which was filed with the petition for an election to incorporate, has a starting point one mile due west from the point actually incorporated. In fact it was not only a mile away, but was in Blount county instead of Etowah County. It was thought best to dissolve the corporation and start anew as the town could never issue bonds or incur outside obligations, nor could it legally enforce its decrees under the old order."*

Altoona quickly filed a new petition and was re-incorporated in 1918.

In 1928 the town implemented public water that piped water from a well at the junction of Main Street and West Highland Avenue. This location was probably a public well years before the public water system came along. The water from this location was pumped to a 60,000-gallon tank on West Highland Street. Customers who bought "city water" paid $1.50 per month. The bills were handwritten on penny postcards by the town clerk whose salary was $16 a month and free water. On May 16, 1958, J.F. Sullivan, H.G. Blanton, and O.J. Sloan incorporated the Altoona Water Works Board.

Original 1928 Water Tank

During this time the town hall was located in one of the buildings across from the bank. From 1928 to present day several things of importance have taken place.

In the late 1920's the town jail was built in the vacant space behind the buildings on 6th Avenue and Etowah Street. This space was sometimes called the "Wagon Yard." It also served as a tool shed and later had public restrooms.

August 30, 1951 saw the incorporation of the Altoona Housing Authority by J.F. Thompson (Chairman), O.J. Sloan, John Thompson, Ellie Foster, and M.H. Thompson.

Sometime between 1947 and 1956, a group of 25 voters submitted a petition to probate judge Wiley Hickman calling to adopt the commission form of government. Either the petition was deemed illegal, or the vote did not pass.

In the 1956 election the first woman elected to a municipal political office in Etowah County was elected as an alderman for Altoona. Mrs. Louise Olson.

In 1957 a $50,000 Civil Defense Mobile Hospital was set up in Altoona.

A new 10-unit housing project was also constructed on Self Street. The project cost was $102,778. Soon after more were constructed nearby.

In 1958 the town used $55,000 to expand its water system. Adding a new well and pump off of Phillips Street. This addition doubled the capacity of the town's water system. An additional fire main and eight fire hydrants were also added. 10,000 feet of service lines to residents was also part of the expansion.

In 1959 Altoona proposed a land expansion to extend the town limits.

It was also around this time that plans for a huge water system were looked at. The proposal was to create a water reservoir and pump water out of the Warrior River. This would provide Altoona with 100 million gallons of water daily for Altoona and the surrounding area. The plan was for Birmingham and Oneonta to guarantee purchasing a minimum amount of water from the system. The Birmingham group rejected the offer and the plans for the reservoir fell apart.

Soon after this a $178,800 sanitary sewer and sewage treatment facility was constructed.

In the mid-1960's four more housing units were added off of 11th Avenue.

In 1972 a $78,460 contract was awarded to build a new 300,000-gallon water tank. Altoona also received a $9,873 grant from the Department of the Interior to add picnic sites, fencing, backstop, bleachers, tennis courts and lights to the already existing ball field and recreational building. The park opened in 1973.

1974 saw the completion of the new water tank, new fire hydrants, and more water lines. $6,000 from revenue was used to purchase a police car, fire truck, and firefighting equipment. Altoona also moved its town hall to its present location at West Highland Avenue and Main Street.

In 1976 defeated opponent Hershel Davenport filed a suit against Mayor Butch Davis. The suit claimed that Davis' service station charged and received excessive prices for gasoline, oil, tires, batteries, lubricants, repair parts and other products sold to the city. Also claimed was a law that prohibited municipal officers from having a direct or indirect interest in any contract or business within the city where they hold office. During this time the town took action by dividing business between Davis' service station and the other service station in Altoona. They case was settled out of court with Mayor Davis agreeing to halt all trading of the town with his service station.

In 1979, 17 residents petitioned the city objecting the location of a new housing project citing it would "depreciate our neighborhood and property value."

On June 27, 1983, lightning damaged Altoona's water pump, making water unavailable. The National Guard brought in two 450-gallon tank trucks and parked them in front of town hall. Walnut Grove supplied the water and residents lined up with containers.

In 1984 it was discovered that Altoona was $32,000 in debt. This was due to social security tax debt, payroll deductions, malfunctioning water meters, and bookkeeping oversights. These debts were paid off in early 1985. Altoona also received several grants in 1984. A $131,439 grant bought 17,930 feet of PVC water lines, and 16 new fire hydrants. $5,000 in grant money was put toward a remodel of the recreation building and a summer nutrition program. The fire hall was moved into the old high school gym.

In 1985 Altoona annexed some 5,000 acres west of town several miles down Highway 132, and continued their annexation of property in 1986.

In 1988 Altoona received an $188,000 grant that allowed them to repave most of the roads in town.

1989 saw the construction of the Chestnut Hills Apartments on Smith Drive. A new police car and dump truck were purchased. Also on October 21, 1989, the Altoona reunion festival was held. Activities included: craft booths, bands, gospel quarters, Indian dancers, and horse-and-wagon rides. The celebration was dedicated to Miss Annie Hendricks.

In 1991 the West Side library opened. This was due to the efforts of a library board, made up of members from Altoona and Walnut Grove.

In 1993 Oneonta signed a contract to buy 300,000 gallons of water per day from Altoona for $9,000 a month. During the blizzard of 1993, the recreation building was used as a shelter. The town bound together and generators kept the public water running.

In 1994 Altoona formed the Department of Public Safety with around-the-clock coverage for fire and emergency situations. Two paramedics were on duty each shift.

2001 was a big year for Altoona. Early in the year the ambulance service was shut down. Because of this ambulance service had to come from Oneonta, 10-15 minutes away. On November 24, 2001, a tornado struck the town. The town bonded together with fire and rescue workers there in service. Many homes were destroyed (including the Altoona housing authority units on 11th Avenue) without any loss of life.

By 2003 the housing units had been rebuilt, water lines had been expanded and natural gas lines were run to several parts of the town. A new fire and rescue squad building was built on the east side of town off of Highway 132. The other half of the building still serves as a community center.

2004 saw the renovation of the park with the addition of a little league field adjacent to the tennis and basketball courts.

On May 8, 2008, A-Med ambulance service was incorporated and continues to serve the people of Altoona. It soon expanded into other parts of the county. On May 10, 2008, Altoona celebrated its 100th anniversary as a town. Groups such as Dollar Mountain Bluegrass, Plan B, Classic Vibe, Ballyhoo and Blackhawk performed. Children had inflatables to play on, with t-shirts, and concessions also sold at the event. Vendors with arts, crafts and other merchandise also set up along 6th Avenue. The Oscar Mayer Weiner Mobile was there as well as a museum set up at Dr. Jenkins old office on 6th Avenue. The all-day event concluded with fireworks.

Through the years Altoona has been host to several fall festivals, spring celebrations, the annual West

City Hall across from bank, mid 1930's.

End homecoming parade, and an ever-growing Christmas parade.

List Of Mayor Aldermen, and Town Officials

1908
Mayor	C.L. Thompson				
Aldermen	B.H. Ellison	S.S. Guinead	J.C. Waid	W.C. Thompson	J.W. Reid
Treasurer	Dr. J.H. Ellison				
Clerk	A.M. Phillips				
Chief Of Police	W.J. Cleveland				
Street Overseer	J. C. Waid				
Health Officer	Dr. J. H. Ellison				

1909
Mayor	James Kay			
Aldermen	W.D. Pope	T.S. Cook	S.S. Guinead	J.F. Thompson

1910
Mayor	L.E. Thomas				
Aldermen	R.W. Saye	W. D. White	W. J. Ellison	L.M. Thompson	Alfred Reece
Clerk	E. E. Scott				
Chief Of Police	L. E. Dean				
Street Overseer	Alfred Reece				

1911
Mayor	R.W. Saye	
Aldermen	R. L. Cagle	W. D. White
Clerk	E. E. Scott	
Chief Of Police	L. E. Dean	

1912
Mayor	H. M. Cornelius				
Aldermen	H. L. Starkey	W. D. White	T. A. Alexander	J. R. Greer	J. F. Thompson
Clerk	A. M. Phillips				
Chief Of Police	W. S. Painter				

1913
Mayor	H. M. Cornelius				
Aldermen	N. O. Hullett	C. D. Ellison	T. A. Alexander	J. R. Greer	J. F. Thompson
Clerk	A. M. Phillips				
Chief Of Police	Hugh Heptinstall				

1914
Mayor	C. S. Ellison				
Aldermen	G. W. Gash	M. Bains	J. R. Sullivan	L. P. Thompson	H. E. Boyd
	W. A. Green				
Clerk	C. S. Hardin				
Chief Of Police	J. W. Baggett				

1916
Mayor	Walker Hale				
Aldermen	R. L. Cagle	L. T. Taylor	W. A. Green	A. McIlquhan	E. E. Scott
Clerk	John Thompson				

Chief Of Police	J. M. Waid
Health Officer	I. J. Samuel, L. A. Kilpatrick

1918

Mayor	John Thompson				
Aldermen	Dr. I. J. Samuels	Dr. E. H. Lindsay	A. M. Mcilquhan	L. T. Taylor	Lee Vines
Clerk	H. L. Gruman				
Chief Of Police	W. D. Lee				
Health Officer	I.J. Samuel				
Attorney	L. Franklin				

1920

Mayor	H.E. Boyd				
Aldermen	C. V. Williams	Lee Vines	I. J. Samuels	J. R. Greer	H. L. Gruman
Clerk	E. E. Scott				
Chief Of Police	G. F. Muse				
Health Officer	I.J. Samuel				

1922

Mayor	J. R. Greer				
Aldermen	John Waymon	John Thompson	I. J. Samuels	C. V. Williams	H. L. Gruman
Clerk	J.N. Akers				
Chief Of Police	G. F. Muse				
Health Officer	I.J. Samuel				

1924

Mayor	E.E. Scott			
Aldermen	R.W. Saye	O.B. Powell	J.R. Bugg	John Thompson
Treasurer	Keith Reavis			
Clerk	J.N. Akers			
Chief Of Police	G. F. Muse/W.E. Graves			
Health Officer	I.J. Samuel			

1929

Mayor	E.E. Scott
Clerk	Troy Phillips
Health Officer	I.J. Samuel

1931

Mayor	E.E. Scott
Clerk	T.P. Bradford
Health Officer	I.J. Samuel

1933

Mayor	E.E. Scott				
Aldermen	J.R. Greer	J.F. Thompson	B.S. Nowlin	W.N. Harris	J.D. Prince
Treasurer	T.P. Bradford				
Clerk	T.P. Bradford				
Chief Of Police	G.F. Muse				
Health Officer	I.J. Samuel				

1937

Mayor	John Thompson				
Aldermen	Harry Brown	J.D. Prince	J.R. Sullivan	W.N. Harris	R.S. Blanton
Clerk/Treasurer	B.M. Thompson				
Chief Of Police	Sam Phillips				
Fire Chief	W.N. Harris				
Health Officer	I.J. Samuel				

1942

Mayor	John R. Greer	(T.P. Bradford starting in 1945)			
Aldermen	Harry Brown	J.F. Sullivan	J.D. Prince	Howard Blanton	Wheeler Clifton
Clerk	B.M. Thompson	(Rex Phillips Starting in 1943)			
Health Officer	I.J. Samuel				

1947

Mayor	Tom Bradford				
Aldermen	Wheeler Clifton	Dr. E H. Lindsey	J. D. Prince	Millard Thomas	B. K. Walker
Clerk	Rex Phillips				
Health Officer	I.J. Samuel				

1952

Mayor	Tom Bradford				
Aldermen	Wheeler Clifton	Harry Brown	Alvis McAfee	James Bugg	J.F. Sullivan
Clerk	Rex Phillips				

1956

Mayor	Millard Thomas				
Aldermen	Wheeler Clifton	Ellis Foster	Louise Hopper Olsen	J. D. Prince	C.V. Williams
Water Board Chairman	Wheeler Clifton				

1960

Mayor	Millard Thomas				
Aldermen	Earnest Burton	O.J. Sloan	Hershel Davenport	J.B. Bynum	George Clifton

1964

Mayor	Millard Thomas			
Aldermen	Barney Scruggs	George Clifton	Hershel Davenport	J.B. Bynum

1968

Mayor	Millard Thomas			
Aldermen	J.D. Prince/Dennis Burton	Jerry Morgan	Kenneth Davis	Hershel Davenport
	Oliver Sloan			

1972

Mayor	Troy Phillips	Kenneth Davis		
Aldermen	Dennis Burton	Howard McCray/Jerry Morgan	Kenneth Davis/Jerry Logan	
	Billy Chaivers	John Gibbs		

1976

Mayor	Kenneth Davis				
Aldermen	Alfred Satrin	Jerry Morgan	Jerry Logan	John Gibbs	Aaron Hutchens

1980
Mayor	Rex Snead				
Aldermen	Bob Thompson	Hershel Davenport	Van Morton	Joe Davenport	Aaron Hutchens
	Bill Chaivers				

1982
Mayor	Jerry Morgan				
Aldermen	Alfred Satrin	James Livingston	Max Hilburn	Jerry Logan	Aaron Hutchens
	Denny Burton	Alfred Sartin	Tommy Foster	Becky Phillips Vice	
Clerk:	Marsha Willis				

1988
Mayor	Jerry Morgan				
Aldermen	Joe Davenport	James Livingston	Max Hilburn	Ronnie Blanton	Glenn Wade Sr.
Clerk:	Marsha Willis				

1992
Mayor	Jerry Morgan				
Aldermen	Joe Phillips Jr.	Dennis Burton	Marston Murdock	David Nix	James Livingston
Chief Of Police	Richard Nash				
Fire Chief	Butch Davis				
Water Board Chairman	James Livingston				

1996
Mayor	Joe Phillips Jr.				
Aldermen	Rex McAfee	Dennis Burton	Dennis Coffelt	Dennis Burton	Greg Gibbs
Clerk	Jean Lowe				
Chief Of Police	Rick Nash				

2000
Mayor	Ronnie Blanton				
Aldermen	Sue Cox	Dewayne Waldrop	Larry Webb	Dennis Burton	Dennis Coffelt
Clerk	Lonnie Lankford				
Chief Of Police	Robin Grant				

2004
Mayor	Ricky Nash				
Aldermen	Steve McCormick	Dennis Coffelt	Larry Webb	Sue Cox	Tony Nash
Clerk	Amy Simmons				
Chief Of Police	Alan Hicks				
Fire Chief	Dewayne Waldrop				
Water Board Chairman	James Livingston				

2008
Mayor	Ricky Nash				
Aldermen	Kenneth Williams	Bill Cowan	Larry Webb	Sue Cox	Van Morton
Clerk:	Amy Simmons				

2011

Mayor	Ricky Nash				
Aldermen	Sue Cox	Kenneth Davis	Nate Livingston	David Jackson	Ryan Cole
Clerk	Teresa Hutchens				

Official Ballot
CITY ELECTION
Altoona, Ala., September 18, 1922

INSTRUCTIONS: To vote for any candidate, make a cross (X) in the left-hand column opposite your choice.

FOR MAYOR
- J. R. GREER

FOR ALDERMAN
(Vote for five)
- O. B. POWELL
- JNO. THOMPSON
- R. W. SAYE
- J. R. BUGG
- E. E. SCOTT
- J. M. HARRIS

MAYOR & ALDERMEN'S RACE 1956

MAYOR:
- T. P. BRADFORD — 60
- P. H. Handy — 57
- O. B. Powell — 29
- Millard Thomas — 71

ALDERMAN
- W. Clifton — 84
- H. E. Cook — 32
- Herschel Davenport — 74
- Bud Dillard — 49
- Sam Dillard — 75
- J. E. Foster — 110
- C. M. Freeman — 55
- H. M. Loggins — 51
- Oscar Morgan — 22
- Nathan Nix — 62
- Louise Olson — 77
- J. D. Prince — 110
- Herman Self — 20
- C. V. Williams — 85

August 1951

THE INDUSTRIAL COMMITTEE OF ALTOONA, ALABAMA

Millard Thomas, Chairman

- J. R. Sullivan
- Rex L. Phillips
- T. P. Bradford, Mayor
- J. F. Thompson
- B. K. Walker
- H. E. Melton
- J. D. Prince
- Wheeler Clifton

ALABAMA STATE PLANNING BOARD

Governor Gordon Persons, Chairman
- C. J. Settles
- W. G. Henderson
- George Wallace
- W. D. Harrigan
- W. O. Dobbins, Jr., Director

Altoona Fire and Rescue, early 1970's.

-Business After 1908-

Altoona's businesses continued to grow after its incorporation in 1908. Below are listings of businesses from 1915 to 1923:

1915: Altoona Cash Store (Grocer)
Altoona Warehouse Co.
J.L. Bachus (General Store)
Miller Bain (General Store)
Sam Baker (Dry Goods)
Banner (Grocery and Feed)
J.A. Bates (General Store)
T.R. Bynum (Lumber)
T.M. Clark and Co. (Rest and Grocer)
Denon and Cook (Rest and Grocer)
B.H. Ellison (Saw Mill)
Ellison Drug Co.
First State Bank
Green Lumber Co. (Sawmill)
Hale Hardware and Furniture Co.
Mrs. W.H. Heppenstill (Milly)
W. Hopper (Sawmill and General Store)
Charles Miller (General Store)
Z.E. Moore and Bros. (Sawmill)
Phillips and Thompson (General Store)
Raccoon Mining Co.
L.P. Thompson (Hotel and Livery)
W.O. Thompson (General Store)
Lee Vines and Co. (General Store)
Wagnon Hardware Co.
James Wheat (General Store)
W.D. White (General Store)
1923: Altoona Warehouse Co.
J.L. Bachus (General Store)
L. Bact (Dry Goods)
Banner (Grocery and Feed)
T.R. Bynum (Lumber)
Cherokee Coal Co.
Cook and Son. (General Store)
H.M. Cornelius (General Store)
D.N. Davenport
Ellison Drug Co.
C.S. Ellison (Garage)
First State Bank
H.P. Hepinstall (Grocers and Lunch)
W. Hopper (Sawmill and General Store)
L.A. Kilpatrick (Sawmill)
W.E. Lecroy (Grocer)
Mcilquham Hardware Co.
Charles Miller (General Store)
J.H. Moore (General Store)
J.P. Phillips (General Store)
J.P. Reavis (General Store)
J.W. Scruggs (Gin and Grist Mill)
I. Sokol (Dry Goods and Shoes)
J.R. Sullivan (Furn. and Undertaker)
Wagnon Hardware Co.

There were also several men who sold insurance through the years, below are the listings for these salesmen:
1912: T.R. Bynum (Interstate Fire)
1923: T.R. Bynum (Atlas Assurance Co., Continental Ins. Co., Hartford Fire Ins. Co.)
Earnest E. Scott: (American Insurance Co.)
Victor B. Sloan (National Union Fire Ins. Co., Pan-American Life Ins. Co.)
1925: W.O. Boyd (National Union Fire Ins. Co.)
T.R. Bynum (Atlas Assurance Co., Continental Ins. Co., Hartford Fire Ins. Co.)
John R. Greer (Mutual Life ins. Co. of N.Y.)
Enoch H. Lindsay (Aetna Ins. Co., Bankers Reserve Life Co., Home Ins. Co., National Union Fire Ins. Co.)
J.A. Lindsay (Aetna Ins. Co., National Union Fire Ins. Co.)
W.M. G. Roberson (Bankers Reserve Life Co., National Union Fire Ins. Co.)
Earnest E. Scott: (Aetna Ins. Co.)

Getting into the 1930's, 1940's and 1950's there is an expansion on the variety of businesses:

Grist Mill: Bob Saye
Barber Shop: Leo Pruett, Luke Dillard, Jess Turner, Earnest (Tubby) Boyd, and Earl Snead
Café: Esto Godbey, Mattie Thompson, Willie Mae Burton, Bessie Parker, Velma Thomas, C.C. Mann and Mary Rowan
Dry Cleaner: M.D. Heptinstall, L.Z. Hinds
Garage: Noah Harris, M.H. Thompson, Arthur Nix, Pinkney Bramblett, A.J. McAfee, Tom Harris, and Wheeler Clifton
Cotton Gins: Farmers COOP, W. Hopper and Tom Bradford
Dry Goods: B.S. Nowlin, John Thompson and the Jewish families, (Rogoffs, Sokols, Cantors and Berlins).
Warehouses: J.R. Greer, and Rube Thomas
Blacksmith: Jim Reed, Jim Moore, Mr. Vickers
Furniture Shop: W.B. Hazelwood
Newspaper: The Altoona Record
Grocery and Feed: Rich Thomas, John Nichols, J.R. Sullivan, J.F. Thompson, J.B. Scruggs, Earnest Greer, G.M. Phillips, Leo Coffelt, Earnest Burton, O.J. Sloan, and Marlo Hilburn.
Theatre: Rube Thomas, J.D. Prince
Shoe Shop: Monroe Harris, John Morgan
Service Station: Victor Sloan, Earnest Burton, Mrs. John Mitchell, and Arthur Nix
Cabinet Shop: Roland Mann
Beauty Shop: Opal Pryor, Emma Murphree, Idelle Pullen
Doctors: Dr. R.B. Anderson, Dr. C.S. Ellison, Dr. Kilpatrick, Dr. Sims, Dr. Alfred Caraway, Dr. I.J. Samuel and Dr. H.D. Jenkins.
Dentists: Dr. E.H. Lindsay, Dr. Findley, and Dr. Goodwin
Druggist: Sanders Ellison, Jesse (Skitchell) Prince, and O.B. Powell
Veterinarian: Homer Dorsett.
Icehouse: Rich Cagle
Hardware: A.W. McIlquhan, W.J. Ellison, Berry Ellison, Charles Brown, Frank Sullivan, Horace Melton, O.H. Harmon, Mr. Lawson, and Mr. Humphrey.
Altoona also had a hotel during this time.

Continuing from the 1950's until today businesses that were present in Altoona: Altoona Sportswear, Lee, Wrangler, Altoona Gas, Allgas, The Altoona Country News, Gibbs Livestock, Outdoor Chair Company, Phillips Paving, Davis Service Station and Parts, Mity-Kwik-Mart, R&P, Altoona Health Care, Anderson Pharmacy, Burtons Food Store, Savette, Greens, Altoona Hardware, a video rental business, The Leather Lady Altoona Salon, Altoona Fitness, Altoona Discount Food, Texaco, Ed Scoggins barber shop, The Pioneer Restaurant, and Steve's Garage. There are probably many more businesses from that time until now that are not listed.

Thomas Realty Company

Hopper Bradford Gin

Violet Prince at Prince Drug Store

Grand Opening of Burtons in Altoona

Altoona Drug Store (Prince Drug Company)
Written By: Tim Hopper

There was a drug store existing in Altoona when Mr. J. D. Prince came on the scene. In the early 1930's and probably many years before, C. S. Ellison (Dr. Sanders Ellison) owned and operated a drug store. It was located just below where the 2nd Baptist Church is today (I believe that is called 2nd Street). Mr. Prince went to work for Mr. Ellison in the early 1930s. In 1933 Mr. Prince bought the drug store and shortly thereafter the business was moved to Main Street on Altoona, where it continued operations until it was closed in 1985.

Prince Drug Company was owned and operated by Mr. Jesse D. Prince (Skitchel) and Mrs. Violet Prince from 1933 until 1985, approximately 52 years. Mr. Prince died in 1970. Mrs. Prince continued the business until March of 1985. At that time she became too ill to continue to work and the Drug Store was permanently closed in April of 1985. The building was given to the First Methodist Church to be used as a meeting place for the youth of the church.

It might be of interest to mention some names of other people who were employed in the Drug Store for long periods of time. Of course there were many wonderful and loyal employees, but those who held tenure included: Henry Griffin, William Willis, Rex Phillips, Angie Cook, Eudell Green and Mary Sue McCray.

Although Mr. and Mrs. Prince owned and operated the Drug Store; the way they ran it, the store seemed as if it belonged to the people of Altoona as much as it belonged to the Prince family. They were thoughtful people; in business more as a service to the community than to make a living. The customer was always right. If a customer asked for an item that was not in stock, although it may not have been profitable, a few weeks later the customer could come back in and expect to find that item. If they received a phone call just as they were closing, the doors remained opened until the customer could arrive. It was never a chore to go to the Drug Store, it was a joy.

In many ways, the Drug Store was the main focal point for activities in Altoona. It was probably the main news gathering and distribution center for local and other interesting news that was of importance to the people of Altoona. It was also the place where kids gathered after school, and the assembly point before and after ball games. It was the place where young men on their first service leave, just out of "boot camp", proudly exhibited their service uniforms.

After church service, people gathered at Prince Drug Store to continue fellowship until time to go home. Throughout the years, although the faces changed, there was always a group of regular customers who met at the Drug Store each day for refreshments and relaxing conversation. It was the place you went to find out the score of a ball game. Posters on the windows announced school, church and community activities. It was the place where workers congregated before going on shift work in Gadsden. Mr. Prince would not think of closing until the car loads of workers had departed for their third shift jobs.

The Drug Store was the main headquarters for the policemen and the night watchmen. If a policeman was needed, one called or came to the Drug Store. If you wanted to report a fire, again, the Drug Store was the place to go.

The Drug Store was the unproclaimed and unsolicited headquarters of the Altoona community. A water leak in the system, a burned out street lamp, electrical problem, whatever the problem, the willingness of the Princes' to accept responsibility meant that help would soon be on the way.

The Drug Store served as a bus station when the commercial buses ran through Altoona. For many years it also served as a telegraph office. Until the latter years of operation, it was the place where the people of Altoona paid their light and water bills.

Town people gathered there to listen to and later watch sports events. As a matter of fact, in 1950, Mr. Prince won a free trip to the World Series between the New York Yankees and the Philadelphia Phillies because of the interest he had demonstrated in baseball by providing a place for people to listen to the baseball games (Mr. Ben Mitchell submitted Mr. Prince's name as a candidate to receive this honor).

The Friday Night Fights could always be seen by boxing fans at the Drug Store. It was not unusual to have 50 or more people crowded around the TV in the Drug Store, watching a Bobo Alson, Sugar Ray Robinson or Archie Moore boxing match.

In general, the Drug Store was the social night spot of Altoona. Mr. and Mrs. Prince were always cordial hosts and made people feel important and welcome.

The Drug Store has been an important part of Altoona for many generations. It is the most singular place that former residents of Altoona mention when talking about their hometown. And it is the first place people wish to visit when returning to their hometown. We all enjoyed going to the Drug Store and these fond memories will remain with us as long as we live. Up until the day it closed, the Drug Store was described as a charming, homey place to relax and enjoy a special ice cream soda or original root beer.

History Of Hopper Telecommunications Company

In 1907 Altoona was open telephone territory. The people of this area asked Mr. Walden Hopper to talk with South Central Bell and get them telephone service. Mr. Hopper was a businessman as well as a large farmer so he traveled to Atlanta to talk with Southern Bell Telephone and Telegraph officials and obtained a franchise for this area. He purchased this franchise for the amount of $50.00. On March 28th, 1908, Hopper Telegraph and Telephone Company was formed. Mr. Walden Hopper and his farm hands started stringing wire from tree to tree. The switchboard was at Mr. Hopper's house and if you wanted to call long distance you went to his home to do so. The first operator was Mrs. Zella Hopper. Walden Hopper used money from the sawmill, gin, and farm to keep the telephone going.

On April 5, 1923 the Altoona town council passed Ordinance 55. This authorized the Walden Hopper Telephone and Telegraph Company to use public streets to place poles and wires.

In 1929, Mr. Hopper started setting poles and restringing wire Before this no real records of long distance calls were kept; everyone trusted each other to be honest and pay for what calls they had placed. All calls were made by hand crank on magnate phones.

Walden Hopper had one son, Wilber Lee Hopper, Sr., who went into the service during World War II. Mr. Hopper's life came to a stop. Thinking that his son might not return, he released a lot of his territory to Bell. By the grace of God, the son returned home, sorry to hear his father had released the territory to Bell.

After the war telephones started to become more popular and the company began to grow. In 1957, Mr. Hopper deeded all of his property and everything he owned to his son. Improvements were quickly made and on March 18th, 1958, the company was incorporated. A R.E.A. loan helped to upgrade service and build an office building to house the central office. The company also upgraded to a dial system instead of the old switchboard crank magnate type. The old house where the switchboard was located was moved out and the new office was built in its place. The new office opened in July 1960. At that time, the company had 865 customers, 3 outside men and 3 ladies inside. A sub-office was built in Snead, making two exchanges 589 and 466.

In 1968, the company started to upgrade and do away with eight party lines. This left four party and private lines. Customers were then able to dial direct. On August 14, 1971, W. L. Hopper, Sr. died. On August 16th. Mrs. Arnell I. Hopper became the new President of Hopper Telephone Company.

On July 22, 1977, a loan was approved by R. E. A. to construct and upgrade to full boundary lines and to make the Altoona 589 exchange all private lines. A new central office and equipment building was built at Walnut Grove and the equipment from the Altoona office was moved to Snead, leaving only the business office in Altoona.

On January 11, 1982, R. E. A. approved a loan to change the Snead exchange 466 to all private lines. Construction began in April 1985 and by the end of that year all of Hopper's customers had private lines.

In September 1987, Ladd Environmental Consultants, Inc., from Fort Payne, Alabama, completed the contract documents and specifications for a renovation in the existing offices for new 2,856 square foot office additions and complete new roof over existing central office building at Walnut Grove.

The new building was completed in October 1988. Customers began to pay their phone bills on the following Monday at the new facility in Walnut Grove.

In September of 1999 Arnell I. Hopper sold Hopper Telecommunications Company to Otelco.

Town Of Altoona Telephone Bill.

Ryan Degraffenridge, Wilber Lee Hopper Sr., Chester Todd and Alma Thompson in the Hopper Telephone Office at Altoona.

First State Bank Of Altoona

On January 28, 1909 the citizens of the town held a meeting to discuss the prospect of building a bank in Altoona. They elected Rev. D.D. Head as temporary chairman and to choose the best location.

On February 25, 1909, with 60 percent of the stock subscriptions being paid in cash the stockholders met to elect its first slate of directors. The board consisted of the following men: L.E. Thomas, A.D. Thompson, Wm. L. Ellison, T.R. Bynum, W. Hopper, James S. Lamb, J.D. Brice, Clarence S. Hardin.

The board of directors then met that same day and elected officers:

T.R. Bynum	President
A.D. Thompson	Vice President
Wm. L. Ellison	Vice President
C.S. Hardin	Cashier

On March 9, 1909 the bank was officially incorporated with the following listed as shareholders:

Shares sold at $100ea. $25,000 initial capital.

Name	No. Shares	Location
Sam Baker	10	Altoona
Wagnon Thomas Co. (L.E. Thomas)	10	Altoona
Ellison Bros. Drug Co.	5	Altoona
A.D. Thompson	5	Altoona
J.T. Thompson	5	Altoona
W.O. Hullett	5	Altoona
James Wheat	5	Altoona
W. D. White	3	Altoona
L.P. Thompson	2	Altoona
R.W. Saye	3	Altoona
Wm. L. Ellison	3	Altoona
D.D. Head	2	Altoona
J.W. Rickles	3	Altoona
B.H. Ellison	3	Altoona
T.R. Bynum	5	Walnut Grove
W. Hopper	5	Altoona
L.W. Ellison	5	Altoona
James S. Lamb	5	Altoona
D.S. Rasco	5	Altoona
Florein A. Hardin	5	Montgomery
Mrs. J.E. Hardin	5	Montgomery
J.D. Brice	5	Altoona
R.J. Ponder	5	Altoona
J.T. Brooks	5	Altoona
J.L. Harris	5	Altoona
J.L. Murphree	5	Brooksville
M.P. Rhodes	2	Altoona
Joseph Bynum	1	Altoona
Clarence S. Hardin	153	Monterey, KY

Two days later the bank opened for business in a rented wood and tin building on 7th Avenue beside the current Leather Lady's shop. Each depositor was given a small metal bank.

By June the bank had deposits of more than $10,000. A year later that number had grown to almost $50,000. By the bank's third year in business its assets had grown to almost $75,000.

In 1922, the board decided it was time to build its own "modern banking facility." The new bank was built on 6th Avenue. It was a brick and mortar building with steel cashier bars and gold leaf painting on the windows. This building is still in use today.

On January 14, 1926, Mr. Coy Shelton started work as a cashier at the bank. Following the death of Mr. Bynum in 1935, Mr. Shelton became president. This was during the height of the Great Depression. The bank was strong enough that it never had to call for financial help. Many farmers were forced to borrow money to make their crop and First State Bank Of Altoona was the place to secure these loans.

In 1936 Mr. Shelton had a "cow, sow and hen program", which continued on for some time. This was a "live at home" program using the cow for milk and butter, the sow for meat and lard and the hen for eggs. Upon applying for a loan of $25 to $50, Mr. Shelton introduced this "way of living" and very few could get a loan without owning these "live at home" necessities.

During and after World War II money became more plentiful and the bank began to grow. Many workers were present during these years. Here is a list of those recorded: Mr. John Spicer, Mr. Hardin, Mr. Shelton, Miss Geneva Bynum, Mr. John Thompson, Mr. Sanders Ellison, Mr. Troy Phillips, Mrs. Troy Phillips, Miss Janelle Battles, Miss Henrietta Battles, Mr. Joe Keener, Miss Florine Humphries, Mr. Bernard Thompson, Mr. Edward Clifton, and Mr. Rex Phillips.

By the end of 1958, the bank's assets had grown to more than $1.3 million. The bank captured the eye of two businessmen from Gadsden: James B. Allen and Jack L. Ray. Together they purchased controlling stock of The Gadsden Corporation, the holding company of First State Bank Of Altoona.

Jack Ray immediately began to modernize the bank's operations. He replaced the old floor-model adding machines with up-to-date counter-models, replaced manual bookkeeping machines with modern Burroughs machines and updated the tellers' cash-drawer system. He added security measures, central heat and air and a modern telephone system.

Like most banks at the turn of the century the bank had teller cages with bars to the ceiling. Mr. Ray had the bars cut in half creating and open feeling in the lobby while still maintaining the historic atmosphere.

The bank continued to prosper in the years that followed. Jack Ray's sons Ricky, Danny and Allen became involved with the business. The Bank's memorable advertising campaigns, (many voiced and even sung by Jack Ray) along with customer service and a commitment to support the community all helped solidify the bank's position in the market.

The first addition to the bank was completed in 1973 and the second addition was completed in 1983. A remodel was completed in 2009. The bank serves as a focal point for different meetings for several organizations that have used the boardroom as a place to meet.
In 2009 the bank celebrated its 100th anniversary and continues serving customers in and around Altoona.

Probably taken on opening day. From left to right: J.C. Reid, Bob Revis, C.S. Hardin, Charles S. Ellison, and T.R. Bynum.

Jack Ray looking at plans during the 1973 addition to the bank.

"My route here is 68 miles round trip. I've been traveling it six days a week for 20 years. The route out of Walnut Grove was 24 miles, but they added to it. I wore out four buggies during that time and am on my 12th car now." - Mail Carrier, Cecil Bradford

-Altoona's Post Office-

The Altoona Post Office was first established on October 18, 1900. H.P. Burruss was the first postmaster. It is unknown where the first post office was located. The original route (Route 1) covered the town of Altoona. Over the years the service expanded to Moody's Chapel, Boxtel, and Hoppers (Route 2), and out to Snead (Route 3). In 1909 Route 4 was added, which extended service to Taits Gap and some territory on Straight Mountain. Lee Phillips was the original carrier for Route 4.

On Dec. 24, 1915 the post office relocated to 7th Avenue, across from the bank.

On October 30, 1939, the post office was once again relocated, this time across the street beside the bank. This building also housed the café.

In the late 1970's the post office was moved to College Street where it remains today.

Below is a list of postmasters for Altoona's Post Office:

Name	Title	Date Appointed
Henry P. Burruss	Postmaster	10/18/1900
Robert W. Robbins	Postmaster	03/29/1901
David H. Crump	Postmaster	07/19/1902
Robert D. Stanfield	Postmaster	03/29/1904
Alvin D. Thompson	Postmaster	06/16/1908
Charles L. Thompson	Postmaster	11/29/1909
James D. Silvey	Postmaster	06/15/1910
James R. Horton	Postmaster	06/08/1914
James D. Silvey	Postmaster	03/10/1922
Jess E. Hollind	Acting Postmaster	03/10/1923
John Thompson	Acting Postmaster	08/29/1923
John Thompson	Postmaster	01/03/1924
Troy A. Phillips	Postmaster	04/25/1936
Lewey Millard Thomas	Acting Postmaster	11/15/1954
Olie Ray Snead	Postmaster	05/15/1956
Norman Alexander	Officer-In-Charge	06/18/1976
Neal H. Mayberry	Postmaster	09/11/1976
Joyce J. Sims	Officer-In-Charge	06/26/1992
James E. May	Officer-In-Charge	12/28/1992
James E. May	Postmaster	01/09/1993
Sherwin Gaines Wigley	Officer-In-Charge	08/10/1996
James W. Ray	Officer-In-Charge	10/09/1996
Charles D. Hathorn	Officer-In-Charge	01/02/1997
Joyce Sims-Matthews	Officer-In-Charge	10/06/1997
Anna J. Youngblood	Officer-In-Charge	
Charles D. Hathorn	Officer-In-Charge	09/14/1998
Pamela A. Charlton	Officer-In-Charge	01/27/1999
Charles D. Hathorn	Postmaster	03/13/1999
Linda Wood	Officer-In-Charge	05/30/2002
James P. Holley	Postmaster	11/02/2002
Jeffery L. Harlan	Officer-In-Charge	06/13/2005
Michael K. Dunaway	Officer-In-Charge	
Janie S. Geckles	Postmaster	12/24/2005

Original Post Office in the early 1900's.

Post Office Beside Bank mid-1950's.

"So far as I am acquainted with the principles and doctrines of Freemasonry, I conceive it to be founded in benevolence and to be exercised for the good of mankind." - George Washington

-Fraternal Orders-

Altoona has a rich history of clubs and secret societies. The first documentation of such was the incorporation of *The Altoona Club* on November 21, 1901. I.L. Brown was president and D.L. Sullivan was secretary and manager. The purpose of the club was to provide a reading room and social place of meeting for the accommodation and entertainment of its members.

Later Altoona established a Knight of Pythias Lodge. In February 4, 1904 an Odd Fellow Lodge was organized and meetings were held every fourth night.

Also organized in February 1904 was the W.T. Underwood Lodge No. 612. The masonic lodge flourished and in 1908 changed its name to Altoona Masonic Lodge #612. The lodge operated in several locations before being merged with the Walnut Grove Lodge.

Below is a list of past masters for the Altoona Lodge:

Master	Year
Henry Meacham U.D.	1904
Oscar P. Walker	1905 & 1906
J.C. Wade	1907
C.B. Haines	1908
Walker H. Hale	1909, 1910, 1911
J.F. Whisenant	1912
A.M. Phillips	1913 & 1914
W.O. Hullett	1915
Archie McIlquham	1916 & 1917
Albert Hopper	1918
J.R. Bugg	1919
B.K. Walker	1920 & 2921
J. R. Bugg	1922
G.W. Roberson	1923
B.K. Walker	1924-1925
J.R. Bugg	1926 & 1927
B.K. Walker	1928, 1929, 1930
W.N. Harris	1931 & 1932
O.B. Powell	1933
Harry Brown	1934
John R. Greer	1935
Rex L. Phillips	1936
Troy A. Phillips	1937
Paul A. Freeman	1938
E.J. Thrasher	1939
W.C. King Sr.	1940
Frank Sullivan	1941
B.M. Thompson	1942
J.O. Dickinson	1943
Howard Blanton	1944
M.H. Thompson	1945
S.L. Self	1946
R.L. Shotts	1947
Roland E. Mann	1948
Enoch Lindsay	1949
Edward Clifton	1950
Clifford Nichols	1951
Eldred H. Campell	1952
Edward Clifton	1953
Frank Campbell	1954

Below is the list of members that joined the lodge during the first 30 years, or 1904 through 1917.
* **Bold** denotes charter members:

Dr. R.A. Anderson
Dr. H.J. Oliver
J.H. Taylor (S.W.)
A.B. Walker (S.D.)
W.C. Thompson (J.D.)
W.J. Cleveland (J.W.)
Thomas Liddicoat (Dect.)
Henry Meachan (W.M.)
W.J. Elliott (Tres.)
W.W. Sullivan (Tylu.)
Eugene Underwood
J.A. Alexander

Oscar D. Neighbors
Oscar P. Walker
John Roberts (E.A.)
H. P. Burriss
Milton Whitley
D.L. Sullivan
David H. Crump
George A. Hullett
Robert D. Stanfield
Oscar S. Goforth
N.S. Clabin
Bing Rosenbloom
Charles J. Cleveland
L.W. Young
William O. Hullett
James White
Jerry M. Chandler
C. B. Haines
Walker Hale
Robert L. Edge
R. G. Pugh
W. A. Bayne
Joe Tidwell
J.E. Goodsin
J.T. Whisenant
T.J. Bradshaw
J.D. Glasgow
Walter L. Little
J.C. Waid
James Kay
Robert Holt
Charlie Thompson
Docks. M. Gofaith
Harvey P. Waits
J.S. Cook
Archie McGlguhan
W.M. Yarborough
Arthur M. Phyllis
Henry R. Morris
C.D. Ellison
Robert L. Stallings
Forest L. Dover
H.M. Watson
J.A. Collier
L.M. Thompson
G.W. Echols
W.H. Collier (E.A.)

Lewis A. Kilpatrick
Sol H. Wood
L.C. Hearn
James T. Riley
Harry T. Turner
John R. Greer
A.C. Moman
Sam Baker
T. E. Cathen
Samuel S. Guinead
Frank M. House
W.H. Edge
W.D. Pope
J.H. Ellison
G. E. Smith (T.C.)
J. Albert Hopper
James Oscar Veenon
W.J. Ellison (T.C.)
J. Ralph Sullivan
Joseph R. Bugg
Elias J. Thrasher
J. H. Horton
Robert Ryder
A.L. Rankin
Newt W. Davidson
Joe L. Jones (E.A.)
Wm. M. Tueadaway
Chas. R. Green
W.L. Chadwich
O.B. Powell
Nathan Joffees
Andrew J. Hullett
Robert J. Huff
Lonnie J. Brothers
Wesley M. Thurman
Martin E. Couey
Bishop K. Walker

List of members that joined from 1918-1929:

Verbon R. Brice
Louis Boer
E.L. Ratliff
Elbert T. Sullivan
James Martin Snead
Joseph D. Vickers

James G. Smith
E.H. Lindsay
Oceola Ashworth
W.U. Davis
James R. Branscum
James C. Reed
John P. West
Lee Vines
William T. Rickles
William G. Roberson
S.S. Moore
W.N. Harris
G.T. Muse
J.B. Kennedy
W.M. Weaver
C.G. Cox
Jackson N. Akers
M.L. Roberts
A.L. Sokoloue
A.J. Rickles
J.R. Ray (E.A.)
L.A. Miller
Noah W. Wright (E.A.)
George C. Hicks
Henry E. Burton
A.N. Burns
J.E. Davidson
William Huston Heptenstall (E.A.)
Geane S. Stafford (E.A.)
J.D. Simmons (E.A.)
John D. Archer
Phelan Sullivan
Robert Earl Nix
Daniel C. Nix
Frank Nichols
Tom Harris
Troy A. Phillips
Rex. L. Phillips
Mel E. Trammell
Chas S. Sullivan
Ralph Vernon

List of members that joined from 1930-1942:

Harry Brown
Chas S. Drury
Wm. L. Barber
Max S. Berlin
William M. Buttram
Paul A. Freeman
John W. Wilkerson
J.D. Prince
Howard L. Camys
J.O. Dickerson
Horace M. Layman
J. Frank Sullivan
Wm. C. King Sr.
James R. Reed (E.A.)
Terry K. Walker
Ernest M. Powell
Rev. H.J. Vaughn
Caleb N. Powell
Mavin D. Blalock
Bernard M. Thompson
Odus N. Claborn
William D. Thompson
D. Webster Bynum
H. Frank Ledford
Raymond Turner
Howard G. Blanton
Sanders Roberts
Thomas Ray Alexander
L. Millard Thomas
Julius A. Cole
Hubert Scott
M.H. Thompson
Joe Louis Hopper
Charles D. Brown
Rev. M.R. Baucher
Samuel Louis Self
Jess W. Owens
James Anderson
Ralph Self
Ralph L. Shotts
James O. Dickinson

List of members that joined from 1942-1954:

Odell Nails
Cecil Nichols
John Harubson
Beat Howard
Homer Galloway
Dewey Dunn
Charles O. Moore
Charlie Elbert Galloway
Joseph Loyd Hill
Alvyn J. White (E.A.)
Sanders L. Sullivan
Kenneth W. Olson
John A. Thomas
W.C. King Jr.
James Leonard White (E.A.)
E.H. Lindsay Jr.
Alvis J. Mcafee
Roland E. Mann
Ernest B. Robbins
Jesse Ellis Snead
Bob Miller Mohan
James Edward King
Edward Clifton
Eldred H. Campbell
James Barney Scruggs
R.C. Hopper
Homer P. Cook
John S. Brown
J.A. Chandler
Dewey Gunter
Hugh Wester
Grady Stanfield
Wm. D. Greer
Frank Campbell
John M. Williams
Thomas L. Baufoot
Theodus Footer
John Luther Dunn
Albert Joe Pruett
Wesley Boyd Pruitt
Fred Newman Payne
Herbert Clifford Nichols

Duard Wiley Nichols
Henry H. Gary
Raymond E. Cosley
John L. Banister
Garvis K. Nichols
Hurman E. Weston
Jay R. Rose
James Edward Brothers
John Ed. Bryant
Olen Samuel Vines
Q.V. Amberson
Clifford M. Burgess
Manwell H. Freeman
Anthony C. Raia
James H. Agan
Wesley Ray Hutchens
James Ray Bynum
Garth Jackson
Jessie Willard Cole (E.A.)
William Nugent
Willie Mack Campbell
Lloyd Phillips (E.A.)
Robert Murphree
Jesse W. Todd
Hubert E. Moore
L.H. York
Robert Paul Nix
Arthur McClough

In 1907 the Altoona Evergreen Chapter #63 was established. In 1942 it was disbanded. On April 6, 1949 it was reorganized with 20 charter members. Altoona has also had many more clubs and societies over the years including Red Men (which was noted for holding a picnic that drew 3,000-5,000 individuals), Rebekah's, Civic Club, Lions Club, etc.

Altoona Masonic Lodge circa 1905.

First United Methodist Church

The First United Methodist Church was founded on April 5, 1903 as the Altoona Methodist Episcopal Church South. The Charter members were: Dr. R. B. Anderson, Aderan Finley, Mrs. Nettie Hale, Walker Hale, Lula Hoge, Mrs. G. A. Hullett, Mrs. L.D. Hullett, R.D. Standield, F. S. Mullins, Levi B. Phillips, Mrs. Ollie Phillips, R. D. Stanfield, Miss Fannie Taylor, Miss Georgia Taylor, Osgood Taylor, Miss Texanna Taylor, Rev. A. B. Walker, L. D., Oscar P. Walker, Mrs. M.F. Walker, Mahaley A. Youngblood, M. E. Youngblood, Ruphers Youngblood, Stanley A. Youngblood and W. S. Youngblood. All of these members were received by certificate of transfer from other Methodist churches.

The church met in private homes and in the local school until the completion of the sanctuary in 1905-1906. It was around this time or shortly after the parsonage was also built. By 1920 the church had a Sunday school enrollment of 93 and a membership of 363. In 1930 pastor W.W. Heflin painted the interior of the parsonage (floor, walls and woodwork) one color: Battleship Gray. That fall church schoolrooms were added to the sanctuary. By 1931 membership had dropped to 301. In 1939 on unification of Methodism the church became known as the Altoona Methodist Church.

In 1956 the name changed once again to First United Methodist Church. In 1944 the interior of the sanctuary was remodeled. In 1954 restrooms were added in the church and parsonage.

Below is a list of pastors during the church's history:

1902-1903	Samuel Van Buren
4.5.1903	S.B. Smith
11.1903	D.W. Ward
1904-1905	L.W. Young
1906	W.R. Eddins
1907	H.V. Waits
1908	W.M. Yarborough
1909	R.C. Stallings
1910	A.C. Morgan
1911	S.E. Maples
1912	R.H. Hartford
1913	H.P. Waits
1914	William M. Treadaway
1915-1916	J.W. Simmons
1917	W.A. Lowery
1918	C.E. Burdett
1919	J.P. West
1920	J.W. Slyer
1921-1922	A.N. Burns
1923-1924	J.W. Archer
1925-1926	R.B. Lavender
1927	J.J. Sandlin
1928-1929	W.H. Pettus
1930	W.W. Helfin
1931	W.L. Barber
1932-1933	R.W. Sides
1934-1936	W.M. Buttram
1937-1938	H.L. Aldridge
1939-1940	H.L. Ledford
1941	M.R. Boucher
1942	W.W. Scott
1943	C.O. Moore
1944-1947	C.H. Bobo
1948	H.H. Gary

1949	H.E. Weston
1950-1951	Q.V. Amberson
1952-1953	S.D. Lankford
1954-1955	Thomas A. Higgins
1956	J.H. Upton
1957-1959	M.S. Palmer
1960	L.J. Fincher
1961-1962	T.H. Francis
1963-1965	W.J. Gunn
1966	Odie Gregg
1967-1969	F.B. Martin, Jr.
1970	J.T. Whitten
1971-1972	Henry M. Louis
1973-1974	C. Hughs Dobbs
1975-1978	Owen G. Hunter
1979-1981	Edward F. Ray
1982-1987	Terry W. Hill
1988-1989	David E. Holmes
1990	Eric A.D. Bell
1991-1996	G. Harvey Beck
1997	Richard L. Saylor
1998	Larry Parker
1999-2001	Ronald W. Echols
2002-2003	Jerry C. Hastings
2004	Jimmy Hall
2005-2011	Jim Fazio
2011-	Joey Smith

-First Baptist Church-

First Baptist Church Of Altoona was organized in 1904 as Altoona Baptist Church. The original nine charter members were: Mr. and Mrs. J.N. Rickles, W.J. Ellison, Mr. and Mrs. J.C. Reed, Cobb Thompson, Mr. and Mrs. B.H. Ellison, and Mrs. J.F. Thompson. The first meetings were held in the schoolhouse.

In 1905, Mr. Berry H. Ellison and his wife L.C. Ellison for and in consideration of the sum of one dollar and other considerations deeded the property for the Altoona Baptist Church. If at any time it ceased to be a Baptist church the property would return to its owners.

The first building was a white two story, frame structure built with donations from members of all denominations. It stood a little to the left of the present building. There were two side doors and a steeple tower with a bell on top. Rev. D.D. Head was the first pastor. The annual meeting of the Etowah Baptist Association was held at the church in 1908, 1931, and again in 1949. Some of the first families who joined by letter and baptism were: Alexander, Blackwood, Champion, Cole, Cornelius, Ellison, Kelly, Lee, Millican, Peoples, Reece, Tidwell, and Wood. Having no minutes for the early years the growth of the church remains a mystery. By 1930 the membership had grown to 203.

On January 11, 1942, the church burned. On the 14th, the church voted to hold services in Altoona High School with BYPU meeting in private homes. They also voted to start raising funds to build a new church. On June 6, 1942, the vote was to appoint a committee to go to Washington, D.C. to get a permit to build a new church. With the permit members and friends once again joined together in prayers and efforts to construct the fine brick veneer building that still stands today. In fifteen months the basement was completed. Services were held in the new building for the first time on April 11, 1943. The pastor preached, "Perform the Duty of It" at the eleventh hour. Dinner was served at noon with the Methodist church joining. Then at two o'clock Rev. B.E Diken, pastor of the Oneonta church preached about "The Church." Rev. Kelley a home missionary to Mexicans in South Texas preached the evening service. A large crowd celebrated the birth of the new church building. Also in 1942 several members left the church to form Altoona Second Baptist Church.

In 1947, during the pastorate of Rev. T.A. Chandler the church started services every Sunday.

The chimes were dedicated in November 1949, given to the church in memory of Mrs. Nora L. Thompson. After 40 years of serving as choir director Bro. J.E Thompson retired. His family gave the original white hymnal books to the church in his memory. A remodeling program was begun in the late 1950's. The Ellison family donated windows and various members and friends provided new furniture for the sanctuary. In 1960 the membership was 197.

During the 1960's, the church furnished a room at the Baptist Memorial Hospital in Gadsden, incorporated to borrow money for an addition to the pastorium, started a rotating Deacon system, adopted the original constitution, let West End Elementary School have use of the building after the school burned, bought a church bus, and began redecorating the Sanctuary.

During 1974 and 1975, Bro. Troy Phillips added pews to the choir and the steeple was placed on the church in memory of Miss Jane Blackwell. Carpet was placed on the front steps and walk and the Sanctuary was carpeted and painted giving the church a new look inside. On November 16, 1977, there was a special dedication service for the RA. Chapel. In 1978, the members sent Rev. and Mrs. Edmondson on an expense paid trip to the Holy Land. In 1979, the basement was remodeled with new carpet and sliding panel room dividers. Cushions were added to the pews upstairs. On October 31,1979, the church celebrated its 75th Anniversary.

In the early 1980's the library was remodeled and the ramp was built in memory of Paul Freeman. Later that year the Brotherhood paved the parking lots and a van was bought. In 1990 the membership had reached 263. The Family Life Center was built and dedicated in 1993. A large porch was added to the front of the building in 2001.

Below is a list of pastors and the dates in which they served:

1905-1908	Dave. D. Head
1909	Rev. Lowery
	L. Lee Hearn
	William Y. Adams
	Steve Rains
	J.M. Floods
	Rev. Solley
1925	J.C. Heptinstall
	John J. Milford
	J.E. Franks
	T.E. Swearingen
	E.J. Lsenhour

1929	R.W. Stuckey
1930-1931	E.J. Isenhower
1932-1934	L.W. Stamps
1935-1936	H.N. Layman
1937	Paul Minton
1938-1943	H.V. Vaughn
1944-1947	Ralph Longshore
1948-1949	Tom Chandler
1950	Raymond Cosby
1950-1953	J.A. Adkins
1954	R.F. Lambert
1955	Rev. Sams
1956-1963	E.U. Calvert
1964	Ed Ables
1965-1967	Charles Underwood
1968-1972	David Homan
1973-1984	John Edmondson
1985-1995	J.D. Brown
1996	Darrin Wade
1997-2003	Mylon Metcalf
2004-2005	James Benefield
2006-2008	Donald Thoms
2009-	George Dunn

-Second Baptist Church-

Second Baptist Church was organized in 1942 with seven charter members in an old storehouse located on the corner of 7th Avenue. The charter members were: Mr. and Mrs. John Nichols, Mrs. Georgie Hazelwood, Mrs. Odell Guined, Mrs. Elvie Maynor and Mr. and Mrs. Phelan Sullivan. Brother Bert Jones was the pastor of this young church of seven members. In 1946, a new church building was built out of block in the present location on 7th Avenue on land donated by Mr. John Nichols. The church was first organized as Second Street Baptist Church but in the early 60's it was learned that the church was located on 7th Avenue and the church decided to leave off the street part of the name.

Pastors serving the church from 1942 to 2002 are: Bro. Bert Jones, Bro. Manvil Freeman, Bro. Bill Ellen, Bro. Jack Bright, Bro. RS. Fox (twice), Bro. Harry McClellan, Bro. Max Barton, Bro. J.D. Brown, Bro. Alvin Fox, Bro. Lynn Thompson (twice), Bro. Doug Alverson, Bro. Don Cason, Bro. Floyd Brewer, Bro. Jerry Mims, Bro. Doug New and Bro. Harold Coe.

While Brother RS. Fox was pastor a sad thing happened to the young church. The church building caught fire one Sunday afternoon. The fire gutted the interior to the point where it had to be remodeled. As the Lord blessed, the small church continued to grow requiring several additions over the years that followed.

The first additions to the facility were made while Bro. RS. Fox served as pastor. A couple of Sunday school rooms and a fellowship hall were added to the back of the church.
Under Bro. J.D. Browns' tenure sunday school rooms were built, central heat and air was installed and a pastorium was built.

The next addition occurred while Bro. Alvin Fox was pastor. Additional Sunday school rooms were built in a separate building at the back of the church. The latest additions to the church occurred when Bro. Lynn Thompson was pastor. The auditorium sidewalls were removed and wings were added to each side to increase the size of the sanctuary. Also, during this time, a baptistery was added and a new education building with a fellowship hall in the basement was built at the back of the second building. The educational and fellowship facilities were renovated in 2000.

-Altoona Church Of God-
(Special thanks to Mrs. Mavis Laughlin)

The Altoona Church of God was chartered in April 1922 in the home of Ophus and Nena Thrasher. Worthy Wilemon was the moderator of this transaction and he served as pastor. The charter members were: Molly Laughlin, Mr. and Mrs. Henry Staton, Mrs. Beulah Brooks, Mrs. Anna Couey, Herman Laughlin, Mrs. Rosa Lemons, and Charlie Laughlin. The membership continued to grow. It was during this time the new school was built and the young church moved into the old school's auditorium, where the BP is located today.

This auditorium filled up with the happy members and the curious spectators, eager to see what was happening. Some came to hear the singing; others came for different reasons. The Great Depression hit Altoona in 1930 but the church kept growing. The old school house was in need of repair but instead of the town decided to tear it down. Lonis Peeples, a non-member carpenter knew that the materials were still good. He told the members that if they could tear the building down without damaging the materials that he would blueprint and build the new church. The building he constructed is the one that stands today on 10th Avenue. The parsonage was built across the street in 1952. Rev. Grady Scott was the pastor and a carpenter. Rev. Scott and his brother-in-law did most of the construction work themselves. In 1948 and 1952 Sunday school rooms were added during Rev. Melvin Ashmore's time as pastor. The large group of teenage boy in attendance that the time help with the construction of the Sunday school rooms. Jewel Murphree, a non-member helped dig out the dirt for this addition. In 1973 the bathrooms were added to the back of the sanctuary when Rev. Roy Cordell was pastor. Money for the project was raised in various ways. Sister Sally Puckett made a quilt to be auctioned off to help raise money for the construction. The interior of the church was remodeled and chandeliers were added during Rev. Thomas Cooper's time as pastor. In 2005 new carpet was added and the pews were covered.

Other churches inside the city limits include: Lighthouse Church, The Church Of God Of Prophecy, and The Full Gospel Tabernacle.

-East Side Baptist Church-

The East Side Baptist Church was erected in 1919 under the leadership of Reverend J.S. Thornton. Deacons were; B.N. Moore, W.J. Griffen, G. Williams, Ike Jones, and Harry White. Later pastors include T.L. Hutchinson, Oscar Cattling Sr., and Moses Foster.

-School-

Education is an important aspect in any town or community, Altoona was no exception.

The first mention of a school in Altoona comes from the September 23, 1904 edition of the *Attalla Mirror*. The paper states, *"Altoona Literary School opened up Monday last with ninety-eight pupils with Prof. D.D. and Mrs. Mollie Ponder will teach us a good school and that is what we need. We have a school here that the west end of Etowah County ought to feel proud of."* This school that they spoke of was a two story wooden building located where the BP's current location. This building was also used as the miners' union hall. The Underwood Coal Company, United Mine Workers of America and the generosity of Mr. W.T. Underwood built it. The second story of the building was used by fraternal orders.

Old Schoolhouse

The April 11, 1907 edition of the *Southern Democrat* mentions Professor Whaley and his assistants Mrs. Ponder and Miss Moore instructed three hundred pupils.

In early May 1907 the following students were listed on the honor roll: Fourth Grade – Vena Wheat, Leola Guined, Charlie Stanfield, Claude Harris, Nina Harris, Hughie Clark, and Annie Hopper.

Fifth Grade – Clyde Mitchell, Vera Jones, Gina Reece, Ethel Whaley, Sumter Smith, Price Stone, Nola Kilpatrick, John Thompson, Gertrude Dunn, and Grace Whaley.

In the September 24, 1908 edition of the *Southern Democrat* the school is mentioned as "Altoona High School".

Due to segregation at the time, African-American children living in the town went to a separate school. This school was first located at the end of 7th Avenue, and then it was moved to the end of Rogers Road in East Town.

The local community supported the schools at this time. The town of Altoona had a school fund that paid for teachers, schoolhouse maintenance, and other school related items. The county also contributed monthly. The following are listings from the town's cash book:

11.11.11: School funds paid colored school teacher one month $25.00

(Etowah County gave a monthly fund for school ($200), Southern Iron and Steel, Raccoon Mining Company Blount County, and Altoona Coal Co. paid into school fund every so often).

11.28.11: Linda Jones one Month teaching $40.00

12.2.11: Clara May Williams one month teaching $35.00

12.4.11: Willie Reed one month teaching $40.00
Leona Shares one month teaching $50.00

12.18.11: School funds for fixing closets $2.00

12.22.11: Linda Jones two months school work $20.00
William Copeland school house sanitary work $1.00

12.4.11: L.G. Coaly ½ month teaching $37.50

1.6.12: Clara May Williams one month teaching $30.00

1.2.11: Willie Reed 3 weeks teaching $30.00

1.6.12: Linda Jones one month teaching $40.00
Leona Shares one month teaching $50.00
L.G. Coaly one month teaching $75.00

2.2.12: L.G. Coaly one month teaching $75.00
Leona Shares one month teaching $50.00
Clara May Williams one month teaching $30.00
Linda Jones one month teaching $40.00

3.1.1910: L.G. Coaly one month teaching $75.00
Leona Shares one month teaching $50.00
Clara May Williams one month teaching $30.00
Linda Jones one month teaching $40.00
Willie Reid one month teaching $40.00

8.3.12: school fund for work on stage $2.00

10.4.12: paid Leona Shares Reid one month teaching $50.00
Onida Holmon Reid one month teaching $45.00
Pauline Arno Reid one month teaching $47.50
D. Henry Pipes Reid one month teaching $90.00

12.4.1913: Bettie Bradford one month teaching $40.00
Clid grey (Janitor) $16.00
Cagle and Ellison coal $4.80

Oct. 1915: Miss Leona Shares $25.00
Ellen Alison $22.50
Prof. J.E. Dean (Janitor) $10.45
Miss Hassie Preston $25.00
Susie Lee McCray $50.00
Jas E. Dean $50

1.1.1916: Bessie Pruett (From Blount Co.) Teaching $10

Nov. 1917: Blount County Journal was used in classrooms 1916-1917 ($2.75 a month)

By 1918 the town of Altoona had removed the school fund from its books.

A new school was built in 1922-1923. To fund this new school all of the miners consented to have 50¢ a month taken out of their pay. These miners and almost everyone else in the community donated money, time and materials for the new high school. The first class graduated from the new Altoona High School in 1923. In 1926 an additional wing was added to the school. The Gadsden Times proclaimed the school as "The most modern school in the county"

At 9:30P.M. on Wednesday March 9th, 1927, the high school caught fire. The fire originated from either a defective flue or a short circuit in the wiring. Citizens saved a few desks but otherwise were relegated to standing by and watching their school burn. The school board estimated the loss between $65,000 and $70,000 with $31,000 covered by insurance. It was reported at this time that the school had 14 teachers on staff.

The school was quickly rebuilt. It was valued at $90,000, had 21 classrooms, a large auditorium, and was steam heated. By 1932, it employed 15 teachers and boasted

500 students. Two busses were used for transportation to and from the school. Altoona also had a dormitory west of the school for housing the teachers. In 1959 or 1960 the dormitory was town down and replaced by a gymnasium that still stands today.

The last class graduated from the school in 1966. It was during this time that Walnut Grove and Altoona were merged into West End. The old Altoona High School became the elementary school. High school students went to Walnut Grove.

In late January 1969 the school caught fire again. The damage was estimated at $500,000, but the school was only insured for $64,000. In light of this and the fact that the two schools had merged, the school was never rebuilt.

-Altoona Alumni-

1923: Lee Bynum
Jamie Maynor
Mildred Boyd
Bert Corneluis
Ernest Vandiver
Lucille White
Rex Phillips
1924: Clyde Powell
Jessie Jo Nix
Fred Turner
J. P. Reavis
Ethel Thrasher
Lillian Nix
Ruth Avery
Arlene Dyer
Jack Phillips
Harley Fulghum
Mrs. W. A. Moore
Willie Saye
1925: Mae Gregory
Gladys Pruett
Fannie Bynum
Ralph Ellison
Pauline Reece
Ollie Bynum
Beatrice Eubanks
Artis Scruggs
Mark Arnold
Webster Bynum
Elbert Nash
Harvey Holtzclaw
Sarah Rogoff
Haye Miller
Mack Horton
Corinne Turner
Marvin Madders
James Reed
Alma Murphy
Bert Bynam
Pansy Nix
Earl Bynum
Millard Thomas
1926: Vivian Bynum
Gladys Snead
Esther Kinney
Louie Bynum
Frazier Copeland
Mrs. Frank Norton
Arnice Snead
Ewell Holland
Addie R. Rickles
Ruth Cain
Alvin White
Vera Boring
Hortense Gilliland
Judson Head
Blanche Reynolds
1927: Elizabeth Boyer
Hugh Boyd
Ara Ellison
Ray Alexander
Paul Freeman
Charlie Freeman
Raymond Neighbors
Beuna Scruggs
Mildred Bradford
Joe Bynum
Loyd Clifton

Grace Wright
Lunie Kelley
Mel Tramell
Eunice Nash
Beulah McCray
Coy Nash
Willene Baker
1928: Lorene Adkins
Hershel Kinney
Annie Bell Bain
Aimee Harvey
Lula Nash
Agnes Kinney
Clarence Alexander
Edward Sandlin
Lucille Jackson
Ada Tessneer
Lela Roberts
Harold White
Maggie Baker
Avil Marie Wood
Keith Stephens
Louie Brothers
C. S. Ellison
Bernard Thompson
1929: Kathleen Chambers
Eldora Foster
Estelle Griffin
Clara Murphree
Lawrence Jackson
Louis Rogoff
Jennings Bryan
Drexel Phillips
1930: Faye Collier
R. D. Collier
Roy Gunter
Odis Jackson
Eugene Blackwood
J. B. Bynum
Ruby Pruett
Ruby Cleveland
Grace Samuel
Minnie Reed
Gretta Hafley
Kathleen Rickles
Terry Walker

1931: Laura Bell Hopper
Eugene Cook
Frank Sullivan
Ralph Atkins
Kyle Thrasher
Gayle Miller
Mrs. Roy Gregory
Dennis Stephens
L.B. Stephens
Mabel Lee
Inez Jackson
Ida Mae Carver
Emmett George
Raymond Smith
1932: Aurella Bramlett
Martha Sullivan
Christine Greer
Inez Griffin
Gladys Smith
Clyde McMinn
Beulah Jackson
Audra Self
Velma Thomas
Drew Collier
Otis Claborn
Ellie Foster
Ross Hopper
Newell Payne
Bobby Self
Elwood Eisenhower
Milford Rennow
William Willis
Sanders Roberts
1933: Lela Alexander
Ida Brown
Minnie Ruth Boring
Mary Lou Boring
Elsie Cagle
Hosea Carver
Howard Carver
Garland Farabee
Mildred Harris
Leon Horton
Nellie Ingram
Thelma Kinney
Clifton Nash

J. V. Miller
Lucile Phillips
Claude Samuel
Grady Stanfield
Eugene Starkey
Lorene Sloan
James White
Billy Jo Freeman
1934: Clarence Bynum
Russell Bynum
Bill Bugg
Thomas Cavanaugh
Lois Collier
Drexel Hopper
Melvin Hopper
Adrian Jackson
Jewell Jackson
Lorene Jackson
Opal Lindsay
Clyde Murphree
Garvis Nichols
John Samuel
Gordon Silvey
Alton Thomas
Evelyn Thompson
Ray Roberts
Julian Wadsworth
1935: Bobby Baker
Ralph Self
Evelyn Denson
L. B. Dillard
Hubert Dorsett
Sarah Powell
Willie Stanfield
Alston Payne
Ola Hopper
Frank Hopper
Billy Thompson
Rhals Sizemore
Randall Murphree
J. L. Williams
Jessie Murphree
Lucille Thomas
Varion Maynor
Nellie Parker
Morris Horton
Dwight Larrison

Mattie Lou Street
Jessie Gash
1936: Ruby Sue Bradford
Charles Brown
Mary Lou Dearman
Imogene Bynum
Theodus Foster
Arlie Jo Farabee
Mary George
Henry Griffin
Juanita Holland
Stacy Hopper
Ruby Jackson
Emma Thompson
Ruth Stancil
Lucille Walker
Nolan Nails
Madge Mitchell
June Moore
Lena Bell Maynor
J. R. Payne
Sarah Thompson
Mabel Self
Helen Starkey
Harry Self
1937: W. J. Bradford
Pauline Larrison
Nellie Mae Maynor
Floy Thomas
Henry Nichols
Joseph Humphries
Grady Payne
A. J. Pruett
S. L. Self
Leon Starkey
Winnie Ruth Wester
Pheron Self
Garold Cavanaugh
Pearl Harris
Margaret Griffin
Evelyn Greer
Lillian Horton
Kate Nails
Nettie Mae Denson
Joffre Ponder
Evelyn Starkey
James Samuel

Gus Buttram
1938: Opal Parker
Raymond Self
Eudell Green
Jim Wallace Hopper
Christine Walker
William Gash
Bennie Mae Mitchell
Anderson Vaughan
Billie Williams
Bessie Ruth Hopper
Tinie Hopper
John Morris Greer
Talmadge Leatherwood
Edith Fore
Opal Gable
Lola Humphries
Inez Maynor
James Dickinson
John Ray McGuire
Opal Copeland
1939: Irene Berlin
George Bugg
Loraine Collier
Dixie Denson
June Dobbins
Christine Foster
Stanley Taylor
Wayne Greer
Florene Humphries
Louise Hopper
Fred Hopper
Doris Humphries
Mildred Jackson
Sybil Jackson
Gladys Nix
Audrey Stancil
Carl Stancil
Edwin Starkey
Earline Silvey
Billy Sizemore
Lilah Hammett
1940: Horace Taylor
Martha Staton
Wilbur Lee Cagle
L. V. Carver

Dorothy Cole
David Cornelius
Pauline Dearman
Lois Golden
Inezalee Hopper
Edith Humphries
Audra Jackson
Ralph Jackson
Alfred Lee
Thelma Dee Nix
Charles Miller
Juanita Phillips
Kenneth Hazelwood
Mary Sue McDerment
Iavae Roberts
Herman Self
1941: D. B. Bynum
Evelyn Berlin
Gloria Dickinson
John Dobbins
Ruby Gable
Jay George
Arlene Hopper
David Hopper
Dorothy Jackson
Vera Kilpatrick
C. King
Roland Nix
Harold Parker
Opal Payne
Maxine Wester
Edith Wilemon
Braxell Roberts
Johnny Thomas
Cora Lee Womack
Gaston Tilley
Eschol Taylor
Harold George
Deimos Roberts
Sanders Sullivan
Johnnie Williams
1942: Durwood Brooks
Talmadge Battles
Edward Clifton
James Collier
J. D. Denson

Howard George
William Greer
Jessie Lee Hopper
Edith Hopper
Inez Keener
Verdie Mae Nichols
Verbom Murphree
Emma Martha Mohon
Imogene Phillips
Susie Mae Powell
Grace McAfee
Florence Gaylor
Inez Brown
1943: Dorthene Ashworth
Virginia Scruggs
Winfred Thacker
Eugenia Shelton
Jeanette Rennow
Mildred Self
Louise Harris
Norma Self
Enoch Lindsay
Ollie Bell Stover
Leon Hopper
Robert Taylor
Marie Golden
Dixie Thompson
Venice Wicks
Wilburn Wester
Paul Nix
Eulice McClendon
Marion J. Freeman
Eugenia Shilton
1944: Geneva Brown
Doris Bynum
June Burton
Evelyn Collier
Imogene Hazelwood
Edward King
R. B. Mitchell
Miller Mohon
Boyd Pruett
M. L. Roberts
Christine Stancil
Irene Saye
Mary Sue Silvey
Lucille Thompson

Betty Campbell
1945: Margaret Brooks
Mary Ruth Clifton
Merlene Miller
Frances Payne
Mary Golden
Violet Smith
Edgar Payne
Laura Lee Hopper
Frances Tiller
Imogene Fore
Viva Stancil
Onzelle Gaylor
1946: Mildred Campbell
June Davidson
Willie Hugh Nix
Frances Thomas
Louise Thomas
Mildred Rayford
Audra Saye
John Dickinson
Newman Payne
Sue Humphries
Doris Jackson
Mary George Lindsay
Valicine Holcomb
Lamar Hurst
Bill Phillips
Iva Lee Hipp
1947: Ray Bynum
James Eldridge Blakely
Jennette
Robert Clifton
Mary Ruth Coffelt
Pauline Cook
Mary Hicks
Virginia Gibbs
Joyce Tyler
Nathan Nix
Jean Mitchell
Gloria Self
Christine Golden
Mary Jo Dill
Marie Hopper
Bert Cornelius
Bert Washburn
W. E. Roberts

Russell Prince
1948: Earl Beacham
Frank Campbell
Eloise Cone
Kenneth Davis
Marilyn Dillard
Pansy Ruth Dill
Barbara George
Aunice George
Virginia Greer
J.D. Gunter
Sarah Hurst
Deward Lindsay
Virginia Lacks
Margaret Keener
Wayne Morton
Walt Miller
Roy J. Phillips
Jr. Phillips
Max Pruett
Carolyn Self
Kathryn Sloan
Jimmy Sloan
Annie Ruth Thompson
Juanita Wester
Adrian Bynum
1949: Minnie Jo Battles
John R. Burton
Raymond Berlin
Alvin Campbell
Howard Clifton
Bernice Eudy
Robert Fendley
Annabelle Hopper
Eschol Jackson
Bobby Ray Jackson
Rolaine Mann
Mary Sue McGuire
Harry Thomas
Margaret Vernon
B. K. Walker, Jr.
Willie Wicks
Jimmy Parker
1950: Edward Clifton
Bertie Lee Canada
Helen Thompson

J. B. Foster
Lucille Fulenwider
Loretta Gibbs
Mildred Holmes
Pauline Henderson
Palmer Dee Jackson
Velma Ruth Jackson
Howard McCray
Harold Thompson
Alfred Mitchell
Joe Henry Stancil
Max Self
Doris Payne
Mary Mann
Bob Sloan
1951: Bonnie Ruth Brooks
Geneva Bell
Kathleen Dingler
Eddie Joe Vernon
Marion Moody
Buddy Humphries
Hubert Wicks
Loy Hopper
Vernell Gibbs
Jessie Faye Eudy
Bobby Wilemon
James Coffelt
Joseph Noojin
Kathleen Thompson
1952: John Wesley Battles
Janelle Battles
Douglas Bynum
James Bell
Dennis Ray Burton
Max Bynum
Alma Ruth Golden
Kathleen Gilbert
Jerry Foster
Barbara Fulenwider
Patricia Greer
Leon Jackson
Bonnie Sue McNair
Jimmy Parker
Shirley Walker
Ellen Self
Ruth Thompson

1953:
Paul Amberson
Doris Barton
Rebecca Bell
Emma Lee Blakely
Myra Bynum
James Brothers
Mary Kate Roberts
Harold Wicks
Shirley Saxon
Mary Jewell Murphree
Patsy Vernon
Nina Jo Prince
Timothy Hopper
Seldon Fowler
Billy Ray Sloan
Martha Jo Jackson
Thelma Davenport
Annette Mitchell
O. C. Hardin
Adrain Smith, Jr.
Gerald Stewart
Baron Hurst
Winnie Ruth McCray
Kenneth Sartin
Mildred Cook
J. F. Dill
1954: Martha Nichols
Sue Smith
Helen Burton
Travis Payne
Jimmy Willmon
Dorothy Noojin
Dean Stanfield
Malcolm Thomas
Joan Foster
Shirley Payne
Clara Thompson
Morris Coffelt
Jan Boyles
Jerry Morgan
Teddy Freeman
Cranston Noojin
1955: Bobby Thompson
Alfred Sartain
DuWayne McCray
Wilburn Davinport
Roy Hethcox
Ralph Lacks
Bobby Stewart
J. D. George
Virginia Hopper
Peggy Bright
Ruby McClung
Frances Golden
Faye Lindsay
Mary Hooks
Martha Sue Echols
Ruth Holcombe
Eva G. Fulenwider
Donald Payne
Glendon Barton
1956: James Battles
Barbara Burton
Frank Cone
Gladys Cone
Ruby Ellison
Margaret Farmer
Ronald Fulenwider
Jimmy George
Peggy George
Mancel Gibbs
Marlene Golden
Laney Johnson
Mavis Murphree
Bill Nichols
Bobby Payne
Carlos Payne
Margaret Sims
Mack Thompson
Peggy Wheeler
Sammy Willoughby
1957: Patricia Alexander
Samuel Alexander
Carolyn Battles
Eugenia Burton
Frank Bynum
Bobby Coffelt
Robert Davenport
Jadell Dunn
Donald Foster
Billy Don Lacks
Donald Laughlin
Helen McNair

Glenda Moody
Ray Nichols
Ruth Simmons
Betty Sue Stanfield
Kate Sue Stewart
Ann Sullivan
Jerry Thomas
Ann Thompson
Lynn Thompson
James Tiller
Jimmy Vandiver
Johnny Willis
1958: Gorman Alexander
Flora Battles
Louis Chaviers
James Cole
Ann Echols
Martha Elkins
Gail Dillard
Larry Fulenwider
George Green
Max Hilburn
Jerry Hopper
Jerry Jackson
Larry Jackson
Jerry Logan
Margaret McCay
Martha Mann
Libby Murphree
Bobby Nichols
Mavis Payne
Delores Pullen
Vivian Rennow
Howard Earl Roberts
Frances Smith
Sandra Thomas
Jimmy Thompson
Nancy Vandiver
Everett Walker
1959: Kay Alexander
Phyllis Alexander
Henrietta Battles
Hoyt Blakley
Linda Bynum
Ray Cone
Jimmy Davenport

Raymond Davenport
Patricia Eads
Vergie Fulenwider
Linda Gilliland
Auburn Hafley
Robert Hopper
Harold Hurst
James Johnson
Nathan Livingston
Eloise Kilgore
Charles McKay
Larry McNair
Clifford Dunn
Charlie Noojin
Dortha Mann
Joan Nichols
Doris Noojin
Morris Payne
Ottis Ray Tiller
Dale Thomas
Annette Vandiver
Sonny Williams
B.C. Yancey
1960: Martha Sue Chaviers
Shelby Jean Clevenger
Max Cone
Sadie Gilliland
Gaynelle Green
Iretta Hafley
Gary Hilburn
S. W. Holliday
Christine Kilsoe
Billy Ray Hyde
Eugene Jacobs
Clyde Jenkins
Jimmy Kilgore
Larry Payne
David Tucker
Darrell Watkins
Wanda Williams
Buddy Wood
1961: Richard Anderson
Max Barton
Don Battles
Elisha Beasley
Grady Bell

Billy Wayne Cagle
Johnny Carroll
Charles Cook
Bobby Ellison
Peggy Foster
Carolyn Gaylor
Joyce Gilliland
Sandra Gilliland
Freddy Golden
Glenda Mann
Dale McAfee
Handy McNair
Jimmy Morgan
Linda Nichols
Alvis Payne
Faye Smith
Sue Sullivan
Frank Thomas
Randall Walker
Betty Wright
1962: Charlotte Vernon
Charlotte Brown
Harold Burton
Ila Mae Cone
J. R. Davenport
Jimmy Freeman
Nathan Gargus
Sandra Geer
Janice Gibbs
Joseph Golden
Allen Green
Gail Hafley
Gail Hilburn
Leon Hill Tilley
Wayne Hopper
Billy Kilgore
Jimmy Laughlin
Philip McAfee
Grant Nichols
Morris Nix
Betty Alexander
Gail Stanfield
Robert Tucker
Juanita Tyler
1963: Jerry Battles
Wilber Lee Cagle, Jr.
Jean Carroll
Jerry Davenport
Brenda Foster
Roger Fulenwider
James Golden
Roger Hopper
Sandra Hughes
Troy Jacobs
Ruth Holliday
Ronnie Loggins
Eddie McArthur
Bobby McGlaughn
Gail Bell
Judy Noojin
Charlotte Osborn
Earl Payne
Ernie Payne
Linda Payne
Betty Lou Pitts
Mary Sue Pitts
Juanita Poe
Jenny Thompson
Lewis Thompson
Bill Vandiver
Ronnie Wester
1964: Ernie Battles
Mary Blakely
Ronnie Blanton
Linda Bright
Roy Bright
Phillip Bynum
Joan Payne Cagle
Danny Chaviers
Brenda Collins
Dale Foster
Janice Cone Hasly
Betty Hethcox
Patsy Holland
Ernie Hutchens
Thomas Kilgore
Bruce McAfee
Sonny Nichols
June Patterson
Anne Jenkins Payne
Corky Pierson
Martha Smith
Mary Smith
Sarah Smith

Larry Tiller
Gary Woods
1965: Jane Blackwell
Troy Bright
Dawn Clifton
Janice Clifton
Steve Clifton
David Davenport
Mike Dillard
Grant Fore
Tommy Foster
R. A. Fulenwider
David Gilliland
Gary Jacobs
Lessie Jacobs
Charlotte Jenkins
Janice Loggins
Capitola McDaniel
Judy Moore
Linda Poe
Carolyn Thomas
Linda Vandiver
Peggy Vandiver
Ann Vickers
Ronnie Willis
1966: Patricia Bynum
Charlie Cone
Peggy Davenport
Linda Gash
Edward Hopper
Rena Jenkins
Charyl Laughlin
Danny Ray Mayo
Frances McCray
Bobby Moody
Danny Payne
Elaine Pitts
Joel Pruett
J. D. Smith
Sherrie Thompson
Susan Thompson
Sandra Williams
Teachers: Belon York
Louise H. Olson
Norman Adams
Annie G. Hendricks

Boyd Pruett
Emma Murphree
Opal Nichols
Doris Campbell
Tressie Johnson
Beulah Thompson
Beatrice Tuck
Nola Murphree
Lila Jack Webb
Annie Hutchens
Nola Murphree
Mary Pruett
Curtis Price
Miriam Robbins
Dora Reed
Corrinne Gibbs
Inez Davis
Wiley B. Robbins
C. C. Davis
Elaine Campbell
L. R. Brown
Lucille Morrison
Eunice Brown
Wynelle Herring
Grace Whitfield
Launa Silvey
Joyce Farrell
Mildred Brasseale
Mary Jo Posie
Charles Brown
Rilla Harvey
Mildred Brasseale
Ernest Ayers
Fannie Bomar
Geneva Self
Hoye Mann
Leatrice Willis
Principals: E. L. Stoker
J. O. Dickinson
L. H. York
Claude Matthews
H. L. Gibbs
Robert Humphries
W. A. Gibbs
Trice Ayers
Trustees: John Thompson

P. N. Hopper
B. K. Walker
Howard Blanton
Ellie Foster
Frank Sullivan
Lunchroom Workers: Mrs. Erskin Puller
Mrs. Ernest Burton
Mrs. Freddie Green
Mrs. Wilber Lee Cagle
Mrs. Willie Hughes
 Mrs. Harley Loggins
 Mrs. McDaniel
Janitors: Charlie Murphree Ed Davenport

-Altoona Sports History-

Altoona has a rich history of athletics. Known as the Choctaws the earliest known sport was baseball. The July 22, 1909 edition of the *Southern Democrat* mentions that Altoona played Walnut Grove in a ball game at Altoona on Saturday. Altoona lost that game 13-4.

In the late 1950's basketball was started without a gymnasium. The players practiced in yards where there were goals and played gamed in gyms at other schools until the gymnasium was built in 1959 or 1960.

By far the biggest sport at Altoona was football. The earliest recorded season is from 1922. Originally the football field was located off of Self Street next to the present day Gibbs barn.

In the early 1950's a new lighted field was built where the present Jack L. Ray softball field stands. Football continued at that location until the schools merged.

Location Of Original Football Field

-Football History-

Altoona Choctaws
Altoona High School
Colors: White and Crimson/Red

Team Timeline
First Team: 1922
1962 - First 10-0 season.
1965 - Consolidated with Walnut Grove to form West End.

Championships
State Mythical Championships:
1954 Birmingham News

Team Records
Seasons: 42
Winning Seasons: 11
Losing Seasons: 16
Most Wins in A Season: 10 (1962)
Most Loses in A Season: 9 (1957)
10 Win Seasons: 1
Most Points Scored in a Game: 51 (10/9/1953)
Most Points Scored in a Season: 255 (1962)
Most Points Allowed in a Game: 63 (11/7/1930)
Most Points Allowed in a Season: 203 (1950)
Largest Margin of Victory: 51 (10/9/1953)
Largest Margin of Defeat: 57 (1927)
Most Points Both Teams in a Game: 70 (11/7/1930)
Last Shutout: 10/8/1965
Last Time Shutout: 11/6/1964
Shutouts All-Time: 70
Been Shutout All-Time: 99

By The Decade
1960-69   43-13-4
1950-59   43-49-3

Longest Running Rivalry
Altoona & Southside Gadsden have played 22 games. Altoona has won 9 games. Southside Gadsden has won 10 games, with 3 tied games.

Coaching Record:

Coach	Years	W/L/T	PF	PA
Ben Perkins	1962-65	29-8-3	705	317
Ray Campbell	1957-61	28-20-2	653	503
Wiley Robbins	1956	2-8	32	137
Bob Coley	1955	3-6	71	112
Dugan Taylor	1953-54	16-4	405	131
Pat Gallagher	1949-52	9-11-2	221	273
Malcom Cheatham	1951	1-6-1	45	170
J.O. Dickinson	1944-46	0-5-1	13	95
No Team	1942-43			
Hal Brown	1941	0-7	18	143
Raymond Turner	1939-40	3-6-3	39	141
Raymond Bates	1937-38	1-9-3	45	286
Forrest Matthews	1936	0-4-1	0	93
Clarence Glover	1935	1-8	32	192
Thomas Harris	1934	2-7	22	144
Heath	1927	1-4-1	18	148

Season By Season Record:

Year	W/L/T	PF	PA
1965	9-0-1	210	76
1964	3-7	91	157
1963	7-1-2	149	77
1962	10-0	255	7
1961	8-1-1	212	40
1960	6-4	148	116
1959	6-4	118	100
1958	7-2-1	153	63
1957	1-9	22	184
1956	2-8	32	137
1955	3-6	71	112
1954	8-2	226	53
1953	8-2	179	78
1952	6-2-1	106	52
1951	1-6-1	45	170
1950	1-8	56	203
1949	2-1-1	59	18
1948	1-3	19	66
1947	1-3	6	68
1946	0-2	6	25
1945	0-2	7	45
1944	0-1-1	0	25
1943	No Team		
1942	No Team		
1941	0-7	18	143
1940	2-4-2	27	111
1939	1-2-1	12	30
1938	0-5-2	20	162
1937	1-4-1	25	124
1936	0-4-1	0	93
1935	1-8	32	192
1934	2-7	22	144
1933	0-5	6	86
1932	1-1-1	6	12
1931	1-1	16	45
1930	0-3-1	13	130
1929	2-3	49	57
1928	5-2	118	33
1927	1-4-1	18	148
1926	0-2	6	51
1925	0-0	0	0
1924	0-4	33	103
1923	0-1	0	13
1922	1-2-1	25	58

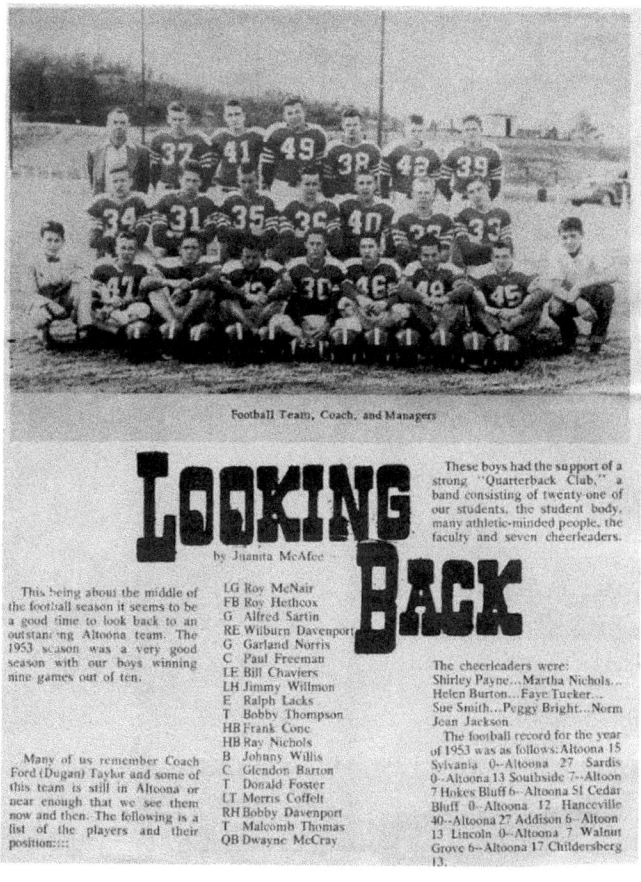

1939 Altoona High School Football Team.

-Appendix A-

Special thanks to Robin Sterling. The following came from his book *Blount County, Alabama Cemeteries Volume III*

Altoona-Walnut Grove Cemetery

Altoona-Walnut Grove Cemetery originally started as a family cemetery. Lafayette E. Bynum is the first known internment. By the turn of the century Walnut Grove had apparently purchased part of the property. This is further supported by the fact it was known as "Walnut Grove Cemetery" at the time. On December 14, 1903, Laura Bates sold 1½ acres to Richard Dobbins, W.T. Underwood, and H.L. Starkey for $37.00. The deed states that the property is to be used specifically as a cemetery. Surveyed 4 Apr 2003.

[surname not recorded, small monument], Linda, 1940, [buried near Silor, Jones, and Self surnames]
Adams, J.B., 27 Aug 1891 – 24 Jul 1892
Akers, Jackson N., 23 Dec 1890 – 25 Sep 1967; SS Naomi C. Akers
Akers, Naomi C., 8 Oct 1897 – 4 Dec 1993; SS Jackson N. Akers
Alexander, Paul, 27 Nov 1912 – 15 Jun 1967
Alexander, Stella, 10 Oct 1887 – 13 Jun 1977; SS T.A. Alexander
Alexander, T.A., 8 Sep 1878 – 14 Aug 1917; Masonic emblem; SS Stella Alexander
Alldredge, Alma Bynum, 8 Jan 1898 – 25 Feb 1978
Amos, Mary B. Wright, 2 Jan 1865 – 17 May 1912
Anderson, [First Name?] 8 Apr 1832 – 19 Nov 1918
Anderson, Clair S., 27 Nov 1898 – 9 Dec 1957; Kansas, Cpl Air Service, WWI; SS Rosa A. Anderson
Anderson, R.B., Dr., 27 Jul 1826 – 29 Nov 1904
Anderson, E.Z., 2 May 1871 – 16 Feb 1949
Anderson, Mary, 8 Feb 1854 – 23 Oct 1910
Anderson, Rosa A., 13 Feb 1912 – 30 Nov 1992; SS Clair S. Anderson
Arber, Clyde, [no dates recorded, homemade concrete monument]
Arber, Tommie Josephine, 27 Jan 1880 – 12 Oct 1908
Armstrong, Barbara Dean, 21 Sep 1937 – [rest of date missing]; SS Walter Lee Armstrong
Armstrong, Mellie Thompson, 9 Feb 1875 – 12 Nov 1934
Armstrong, Walter Lee, 28 Jun 1935 – 25 Jan 1978; MSgt US Marine Corps, Vietnam; SS Barbara Dean Armstrong
Arnold, Ada King, wife of M.L. Arnold, 15 Jul 1868 – 24 Oct 1901, [Marcus L. Arnold married Ada King 14 Sep 1890, Blount County]
Arnold, Arnett, 19 Apr 1893 – 24 Sep 1925
Arnold, Effie, daughter of W.J. and S.E. Arnold, 21 Mar 1883 – 23 May 1899

Arnold, Emmett Sloan, 2 Dec 1918 – 24 Dec 1955; Alabama, HMC US Navy, WWII
Arnold, Emmett, 4 Jun 1941, [only date recorded]; Alabama Mech. 1 Pioneer Inf.
Arnold, Ernest, son of W.J. and S.E. Arnold, 5 Nov 1878 – 12 Jan 1898
Arnold, Marcus L., 30 Jun 1859 – 28 Nov 1909, [Marcus L. Arnold married Ada King 14 Sep 1890, Blount County]
Arnold, Mark L., 17 Feb 1900 – 15 Jan 1955
Arnold, Pauline, 30 Sep 1885 – 19 Oct 1970
Arnold, Sarah E., 1 Jan 1854 – 17 Aug 1941; SS William J. Arnold
Arnold, Walker, 20 May 1891 – 24 Jul 1928
Arnold, William J., 1 Jul 1854 – 4 May 1914; SS Sarah E. Arnold
Arnold, Zora B., 4 Dec 1898 – 10 Oct 1967
Bachus, J. Tracy, 3 Dec 1909 – 8 Dec 1988; SS Opal M. Bachus
Bachus, James E., 1867 – 1949; SS Minnie G. Bachus
Bachus, Marjorie Ann, 11 Feb 1932 – 21 Mar 1933
Bachus, Minnie G., 1876 – 1965; SS James E. Bachus
Bachus, Opal M., 10 Jul 1910 – 19 Dec 1983; SS J. Tracy Bachus
Baggett, J.W., 9 May 1875 – 11 Dec 1922
Baggett, Lellah May, daughter of J.W. and M.J. Baggett, 8 Nov 1897 – 7 Dec 1912
Barton, Elzie W., 21 Dec 1914 – 25 Nov 1997; SS J.T. Barton
Barton, J.T., 30 Apr 1912 – 22 May 1985; SS Elzie W. Barton
Bates, Cora, 17 Nov 1902 – 9 Jun 1904
Bates, F.M., 9 Oct 1876 – 31 Dec 1909, [broken monument]
Bates, Lillie, 21 Feb 1902 – 1 Feb 1910
Baugh, Lawayne, 17 Jan 1948 – [rest of date missing]; SS Mary Walls Baugh; married 30 Jun 2002
Baugh, Mary Walls, 4 Aug 1940 – 9 Jul 2002; US Air Force; SS Lawayne Baugh; married 30 Jun 2002
Beacham, Doris Jean, 4 Feb 1935 – 20 Apr 1994; SS Earl J. Beacham; married 13 Feb 1954
Beacham, Earl J., 27 Jul 1930 – [rest of date missing]; SS Doris Jean Beacham; married 13 Feb 1954
Beacham, Homer Alexander, 15 Sep 1899 – 27 Jul 1990
Beacham, James C., 17 Aug 1932 – 28 Jun 1992; AD3 US Navy, Korea
Beacham, Marvin Earl, 16 Aug 1902 – 28 Jun 1988
Beacham, Nancy F., 3 May 1907 – 6 Oct 1973
Beasley, David, 30 Dec 1927 – 31 Dec 1927; [homemade concrete monument]
Beasley, Edgar D., 2 Oct 1901 – 2 Sep 1985; SS Vera E. Beasley
Beasley, Edgar L., 20 Jan 1930 – 3 Nov 1996; SS Louise J. Beasley; married 21 Oct 1950
Beasley, J.H. Fred, 9 Jan 1925 – 26 Nov 1989; SS Vera Beasley
Beasley, John A., 25 Oct 1927 – 8 Oct 1972; SS Martha A. Beasley
Beasley, Larry Wayne, 29 Aug 1955 – 2 Oct 1991; SS Patricia Gayle Beasley; married 23 Mar 1977
Beasley, Louise J., 22 Sep 1936 – [rest of date missing]; SS Edgar L. Beasley; married 21 Oct 1950
Beasley, Martha A., 8 Oct 1932 – [rest of date missing]; SS John A. Beasley
Beasley, Patricia Gayle, 18 Feb 1957 – [rest of date missing]; SS Larry Wayne Beasley; married 23 Mar 1977
Beasley, Vera E., 27 Jul 1907 – 15 Nov 1990; SS Edgar D. Beasley
Beasley, Vera, 30 May 1921 – [rest of date missing]; SS J.H. Fred Beasley
Bell, Mary Ellen Beasley, 3 Apr 1956 – 9 Apr 1988
Benjamin, Vivian Bynum, 19 Mar 1908 – 23 Apr 1991
Berry, Alice N., 14 Mar 1868 – [rest of date missing, never inscribed]; SS James N. Berry
Berry, Hazel, daughter of J.N. and N.A. Berry, 9 Dec 1903 – 16 Jan 1904
Berry, Howard J., 10 Jun 1920 – 15 Sep 1921
Berry, James C., 30 Jan 1887 – 22 Aug 1926
Berry, James N., 15 Jun 1863 – 4 Feb 1930; SS Alice N. Berry
Berry, John M., son of J.N. and N.A. Berry, 18 Apr 1883 – 13 Jan 1904
Berry, Mary, infant daughter of Mr. and Mrs. James C. Berry, [no dates recorded]
Beshears, Ara Jones, 23 Jul 1923 – 9 Dec 1988; SS Reuben H. Behsears; married 21 Mar 1939
Beshears, Reuben H., 24 Feb 1919 – [rest of date missing]; SS Ara Jones Beshears; married 21 Mar 1939
Beshears, Travis H., 18 Apr 1943 – 2 Oct 1994
Blackwell, Jane, 30 Jun 1947 – 5 Mar 1974
Blackwell, Mildred, 3 Dec 1927 – 13 Aug 1999
Blackwood, Byron Odell, 7 Nov 1921 – 13 Sep 1996; SS Nellwin Love Blackwood
Blackwood, Nellwin Love, 3 Jun 1924 – 20 May 1995; SS Byron Odell Blackwood
Blanton, Myrtis K., 20 Mar 1895 – 8 Mar 1985

Bolden (?), [first name missing], 1868 – 1955, [hand carved monument; dates are best guess]
Bowen, Arminta, 1870 – 1957; SS George W. Bowen
Bowen, Daughter, of G.W. and Minto Bowen, 21 Apr 1907 – 6 Nov 1907
Bowen, George W., 1877 – [rest of date missing]; SS Arminta Bowen
Bowman, R.W., Rev., 9 Nov 1851 – 1 Jul 1920
Boyd, Billy J., 7 Jun 1932 – 14 Apr 1935
Boyd, C.A., 10 Dec 1872 – 31 Aug 1933
Boyd, Fanie, 14 Sep 1903 – 5 Mar 1943
Boyd, Gertie A., wife of J.B. Boyd, 30 Jan 1897 – 14 Feb 1918
Boyd, Joe, 8 Dec 1894 – 31 Mar 1950
Boyles, Bain, 29 Dec 1910 – 16 Jun 1979
Boyles, E.C., 22 Dec 1880 – 6 Aug 1965; SS Lula Boyles
Boyles, Lula, 21 Oct 1884 – 17 Sep 1978; SS E.C. Boyles
Boyles, Miss Willard H., 1909 – 1994, [funeral home marker]
Boyles, Weedon C., 13 Mar 1913 – 22 Jan 1977; Tec 5 US Army, WWII
Bradford, Billy F., 16 Dec 1921 – 27 Dec 1986; Masonic emblem; SS Rosemary T. Bradford
Bradford, Cecil E., 21 Aug 1889 – 8 Jun 1983; Masonic emblem; SS Hattie S. Bradford
Bradford, Hattie S., 25 Aug 1891 – 8 Jul 1981; SS Cecil E. Bradford
Bradford, Isaac L., 7 Sep 1869 – 30 Nov 1948; SS Mary F. Bradford
Bradford, Mary F., 13 Apr 1873 – 9 Feb 1945; SS Isaac L. Bradford
Bradford, Reeda Story, 22 Sep 1896 – 16 Jan 1984; SS Thomas P. Bradford
Bradford, Rosemary T., 5 Oct 1927 – 11 Jun 2001; SS Billy F. Bradford
Bradford, Thomas P., 23 Aug 1893 – 13 Feb 1972; Alabama Pvt US Army, WWI; SS Reeda Story Bradford
Bradford, W.J., 19 Oct 1875 – 30 Dec 1924; Masonic emblem
Bradford, William J., 7 Aug 1917 – 20 Oct 1979; Tec 4 US Army, WWII
Bradley, Hazel V., 3 Jan 1938 – [rest of date missing]; SS Norman E. Bradley; married 20 May 1955
Bradley, Norman E., 12 Jun 1937 – 21 Mar 1993; SS Hazel Bradley; married 20 May 1955
Bramblett, Carol L., 9 Jan 1943 – [rest of date missing]; SS Roger D. Bramblett
Bramblett, Gladys O., 16 Jul 1916 – 4 Mar 1986; SS William P. Bramblett
Bramblett, Onzelle Gaylor, 8 Aug 1925 – 4 Jul 1945
Bramblett, Roger D., 16 Jan 1939 – 31 May 1996; SS Carol L. Bramblett
Bramblett, William P., 30 Oct 1910 – 25 Oct 1994; S2 US Navy, WWII; SS Gladys O. Bramblett
Branham, Fannie L. Taylor, 20 May 1887 – 20 Jun 1955; SS James Monroe Branham
Branham, James Monroe, 11 Jul 1885 – 15 May 1951; SS Fannie L. Taylor Branham
Brasswell, Rohnwyn Essie, 13 Oct 1916 – 24 Oct 1916
Bratt__ [part of surname missing], Martha, Oct 1857 – 7 Jan 1899, [broken monument]
Brooks, Dennis Leldon, 20 Apr 1914 – 5 Feb 1991; S1 US Navy, WWII; SS Edna Ashmore Brooks
Brooks, Edna Ashmore, 12 Jul 1920 – 22 Nov 1990; SS Dennis Leldon Brooks
Brown, Annie E., 1889 – 1964; SS Harry Brown
Brown, Charles L., 24 Nov 1919 – 20 Mar 1998
Brown, Eunice S., 11 Jan 1913 – 29 May 1974; SS Lee Roy Brown
Brown, Harry, 1879 – 1965; Masonic emblem; SS Annie E. Brown
Brown, Harry, Jr., 10 Jun 1928 – 16 Jan 1929
Brown, James V., 23 Dec 1902 – 17 Dec 1972; SS Lula Patterson Brown
Brown, John H., 28 Sep 1869 – 28 Dec 1944; SS Lillie L. Brown
Brown, John S., 24 Oct 1925 – 29 Mar 1997; US Navy, US Air Force
Brown, Lee Roy, 30 Jan 1901 – 8 Apr 1968; SS Eunice S. Brown
Brown, Lillie L., 14 Aug 1872 – 12 Jan 1963; SS John H. Brown
Brown, Lula Patterson, 13 Sep 1887 – 7 Oct 1972; SS James V. Brown
Broyles, Carl Gene, 15 Oct 1941 – 4 Feb 2000; SS Rita Ann Broyles
Broyles, Rita Ann, 15 Oct 1943 – [rest of date missing]; SS Carl Gene Broyles
Bryan, Ollie Rankin, 27 Oct 1900 – 24 Mar 1969
Bryant, Irene Norris, 10 Aug 1911 – 22 Jan 1983
Bryant, J.C., 31 Mar 1930 – 8 Jun 1997; US Navy, Korea
Bryant, Sam, 1905 – 1948
Bryant, Silas P., 1875 – 1956; SS Virginia K. Bryant
Bryant, Virginia K., 1881 – 1930; SS Silas P. Bryant
Buchanan, Fred, 18 Mar 1899 – 15 Dec 1943; SS Parlee Buchanan

Buchanan, Mary Frances, 14 Jan 1883 – 19 Aug 1974; SS William Andrew Buchanan
Buchanan, Parlee, 17 Jun 1912 – 10 Jun 1996; SS Fred Buchanan
Buchanan, William Andrew, 28 Jul 1879 – 10 Sep 1946; SS Mary Frances Buchanan
Bugg, Hattie K., 1885 – 1977; SS Joseph R. Bugg
Bugg, James M., 1869 – 1962
Bugg, Jodi, son of J.R. and Harrie R. Bugg, 25 May 1912 – 28 Jun 1912
Bugg, Joseph R., 1879 – 1929; Masonic emblem; SS Hattie K. Bugg
Bullard, J.L., 20 Sep 1910 – 17 Jul 1933
Bullard, Lester, 26 Mar 1881 – 2 Sep 1965; SS Tenie Bullard
Bullard, Tenie, 1 Apr 1885 – 5 Jul 1974; SS Lester Bullard
Burks, Bill, 9 Jul 1929 – 5 May 1988; SS Mary Lee Burks
Burks, Mary Lee, 29 Jun 1929 – 31 Jan 1999; SS Bill Burks
Burton, Eanoch R., 1 May 1898 – 4 Mar 1961; WWI
Burton, Ernest K., 25 May 1911 – 4 Sep 1972
Burton, Montgomery, 20 Feb 1889 – 8 Jan 1965; Alabama, Pvt Co I 156 Depot Brigade, WWI
Butts, Eric and Dereck, twin sons of Mr. and Mrs. Donnie Butts, 11 Nov 1976 – 11 Nov 1976
Butts, Kelly Diane, 3 Jul 1972 – 4 Jul 1972
Butts, Ronnie J., 5 Jan 1956 – 4 May 1983
Bynum, Agnes L., 17 Oct 1909 – 5 Oct 1987; SS Earl L. Bynum
Bynum, Albert, son of J.A. and Dona Bynum, 7 Sep 1920 – 22 Jun 1922
Bynum, Bertie M., 22 Oct 1908 – [rest of date missing]; SS James B. Bynum
Bynum, Dessie, daughter of J.E. and Genoa Bynum, 16 Feb 1897 – 10 Nov 1898; SS Ruth Bynum
Bynum, Earl L., 10 Oct 1903 – 4 Feb 1951; SS Agnes L. Bynum
Bynum, Fred E., 24 Apr 1894 – 26 Feb 1986; PFC US Army, WWI
Bynum, Genoa Hamilton, 29 Dec 1876 – 20 Mar 1944; SS James E. Bynum
Bynum, George C., son of T.R. and P.E. Bynum, 1893 – 1912
Bynum, Infant, son of T.R. and P.E. Bynum, 1902 – 1903
Bynum, Jacob B., 3 May 1872 – 28 Oct 1949; SS Nora A. Bynum
Bynum, James B., 25 May 1910 – 21 Jun 1989; SS Bertie M. Bynum
Bynum, James E., 12 Jul 1866 – 24 Mar 1902; Masonic emblem; SS Genoa Hamilton Bynum
Bynum, James S., 27 Mar 1859 – 17 Aug 1926
Bynum, John C., 13 Jun 1858 – 12 Feb 1872, [hand carved flat monument slab]
Bynum, Lafayette, 20 Jul 1845 – 30 Aug 1868, [faded monument, difficult to read], [Lafayette Bynum married Susanna Field 25 May 1865, Blount County]
Bynum, Nellie J., 10 Nov 1917 – [rest of date missing]; SS Russell H. Bynum
Bynum, Nora A., 11 Sep 1875 – 18 Dec 1963; SS Jacob B. Bynum
Bynum, Pinkie H., 16 Feb 1870 – 24 Dec 1946
Bynum, Russell H., 5 Jun 1914 – 18 Apr 1997; SS Nellie J. Bynum
Bynum, Ruth, daughter of J.E. and Genoa Bynum, 4 Apr 1892 – 31 Oct 1898; SS Dessie Bynum
Bynum, T.R., 29 Jan 1868 – 5 Aug 1935
Bynum, Velma S., 15 Oct 1900 – 21 Oct 1964
Bynum, Wiley Lafayette, son of Lafayette and Susan E. Bynum, 6 Aug 1868 – 20 Feb 1881
Cagle, Carl, 21 Mar 1912 – 11 Oct 1967; Masonic emblem
Cagle, Clarence, 14 Aug 1900 – 11 May 1970; SS Cleo M. Cagle
Cagle, Cleo M., 24 Jan 1903 – 27 Mar 1976; SS Clarence Cagle
Cagle, Estelle, 26 Feb 1926 – [rest of date missing]; SS Weedy Cagle
Cagle, Richard L., 14 Apr 1871 – 24 Sep 1938; SS Sallie M. Cagle
Cagle, Sallie M., 7 Jun 1872 – 21 Dec 1920; SS Richard L. Cagle
Cagle, Thelma, 8 Jul 1924 – 27 Apr 1989
Cagle, Wilber L. "Weedy," 25 Aug 1922 – 9 Oct 1988; Tec 5, US Army, WWII; SS Estelle Cagle
Cain, Elizabeth Freeman, 15 Sep 1870 – 26 Mar 1943
Cain, Joseph, 15 Jan 1861 – 6 Feb 1955
Caldwell, Elsie Louise Robbins, 19 May 1912 – 5 Mar 2002; SS Tyrus Raymond
Caldwell, Tyrus Raymond, 16 Apr 1909 – 23 Mar 1996; SS Elise Louise Robbins Caldwell
Camp, Infant, son of Edward and Cynthia Camp, 18 May 1899, [only date recorded]
Campbell, Anna Penny, wife of J.T. Campbell, 13 Mar 1851 – 28 Jul 1904
Campbell, Bertha M., 27 Jul 1908 – 17 Oct 1975; SS James E. Campbell
Campbell, Edward Little, 20 Oct 1920 – [rest of date missing]; SS Vera Arkie Campbell
Campbell, Emma Penny, 4 Aug 1886 – 27 Feb 1962

Campbell, James E., 6 Sep 1905 – 28 Mar 1954; SS Bertha M. Campbell
Campbell, Jesse T., 19 Jun 1851 – 5 Jun 1920; Masonic emblem
Campbell, Vera Arkie, 30 May 1910 – 16 Feb 1997; SS Edward Little Campbell
Camper, Donald Ray, 3 Sep 1939 – 26 Jul 1993
Casey, Sara Anniece, daughter of Frank and Christine Casey, 17 May 1925 – 13 Sep 1927
Chappell, Clarence E., 10 Oct 1939 – 7 Apr 2000
Chappell, Ernest C., 25 Dec 1904 – 29 Apr 1969
Chappell, Lonnie D., 22 Jul 1882 – 28 Feb 1960; SS Lucious W. Chappell
Chappell, Lora, 9 Oct 1912 – 4 Apr 1986; SS Marvin Chappell
Chappell, Lucious W., 6 Apr 1878 – 5 May 1943; SS Lonnie D. Chappell
Chappell, Marvin, 14 Feb 1907 – 1 Feb 1983; SS Lora Chappell
Chaviers, Annie M., 28 Nov 1903 – 29 Oct 1992; SS Marion A. Chaviers
Chaviers, Billy Ray, 12 Apr 1936 – 7 Apr 1999; SS Carolyn June Chaviers; married 13 Feb 1955
Chaviers, Carolyn June, 29 Jun 1939 – [rest of date missing]; SS Billy Ray Chaviers; married 13 Feb 1955
Chaviers, Marion A., 6 Mar 1901 – 6 Oct 1975; SS Annie M. Chaviers
Chaviers, Robert Daniel, 23 Apr 1946 – 23 Oct 1987
Cheaves, Jimmy, 7 Jul 1914 – 22 Apr 1948; SS Ollie Vae Cheaves; married 29 Aug 1939
Cheaves, Ollie Vae, 23 Nov 1923 – [rest of date missing]; SS Jimmy Cheaves; married 20 Aug 1939
Clark, Alvin J., 21 Nov 1918 – 19 Sep 1994; SS Pearl Marie Clark
Clark, Pearl Marie, 29 Aug 1921 – [rest of date missing]; SS Alvin J. Clark
Clay, Emma C., 16 Oct 1847 – 3 Oct 1905
Clay, Emma Lawson, 16 Oct 1847 – 3 Oct 1905
Clay, H. Radford, 1888 – 1918; SS Rose Gibson Clay
Clay, Jessie, 20 Apr 1909 – 19 Sep 1909
Clay, Joe, son of R.G. and Lillie Clay, 1 Jul 1920 – 14 Jun 1923
Clay, John Alma, 27 Jun 1903 – 2 Apr 1995; Masonic emblem; SS Mary J. Clay
Clay, Lillie Frix, 17 Jan 1893 – 10 May 1927
Clay, Mary J., 21 Mar 1911 – 1 Nov 1993; SS John Alma Clay
Clay, Nell M., 28 May 1910 – 10 Jun 1987
Clay, Rose Gibson, 1888 – 1972; SS H. Radford Clay
Clay, William J., 25 Aug 1917 – 14 Nov 1960
Cleveland, Arnold B., 17 Nov 1897 – 26 Dec 1973; SS Myrtle Morgan Cleveland
Cleveland, Arnold B., Jr., 17 Dec 1935 – 26 Apr 1998
Cleveland, Callie, 1876 – 1934; SS J.W. Cleveland
Cleveland, Howard W., 28 Aug 1898 – 9 Apr 1985; SS Vonnie Cleveland
Cleveland, J.W., 1874 – 1955; SS Callie Cleveland
Cleveland, Mary E., 11 Dec 1908 – 3 Mar 1993
Cleveland, Myrtle Morgan, 6 Apr 1902 – 2 Oct 1981; SS Arnold B. Cleveland
Cleveland, Vonnie, 28 Nov 1912 – 22 May 2000; SS Howard W. Cleveland
Cleveland, Wilbur, 19 Apr 1873 – 20 Mar 1943; Masonic emblem
Cleveland, William Lonnie, 21 Mar 1895 – 15 Jun 1964
Clevenger, Mary, 9 Apr 1886 – 13 Nov 1976; SS Thomas M. Clevenger
Clevenger, Thomas M., 24 Apr 1875 – 12 Apr 1943; SS Mary Clevenger
Clifton, Infant, son of Susan and Steve Clifton, 30 Jan 1969, [only date recorded]
Cockrell, Henry Allen, 26 Dec 1925 – 9 Oct 1984; S2 US Navy, WWII
Coffelt, Deamie, 13 May 1907 – 13 Jul 1977; SS James E. Coffelt
Coffelt, Frances A., 24 Mar 1901 – 23 Aug 1976; SS Leo E. Coffelt
Coffelt, Frances, 9 Jan 1941 – [rest of date missing]; SS Jimmy Dean Coffelt
Coffelt, George M., 19 Oct 1934 – 7 Jul 1977; SS Mary S. Coffelt
Coffelt, Infants, [no dates recorded]
Coffelt, James E., 17 Dec 1902 – 12 Jul 1969; SS Deamie Coffelt
Coffelt, Jimmy Dean, 5 Sep 1932 – 15 Apr 2001; SS Frances Coffelt
Coffelt, Joseph Harold, 5 Apr 1937 – 8 Oct 1977
Coffelt, Leo E., 6 Jun 1898 – 10 Oct 1984; SS Frances A. Coffelt
Coffelt, Mary S., 10 Apr 1941 – [rest of date missing]; SS George M. Coffelt
Cole, Alfred D., 1848 – 1892; SS Sara Ann Cole
Cole, Arminda, 1877 – 1902
Cole, Artie L., 1883 – 1899

Cole, Belle, 1900 – 1975; SS Julius A. Cole
Cole, Carolina, wife of W.K. Cole, 30 Aug 1852 – 4 Oct 1912
Cole, Emily Armindy, 12 Feb 1854 – 27 Jun 1927
Cole, John H., 1888 – 1907
Cole, Julius A., 1890 – 1966; SS Bell Cole
Cole, Sara Ann, 1850 – 1909; SS Alfred C. Cole
Cole, Sarah Ann, 12 Aug 1856 – 10 Jul 1928
Cole, W.K., 5 May 1885 – 9 Sep 1956
Cole, W.K., husband of Carolina Cole, 30 Jan 1849 – 9 Mar 1897
Collier, J.A., 11 Aug 1882 – 4 Mar 1954; Masonic emblem
Collier, Merceel, 22 May 1898 – 5 Mar 1965
Collier, Roy L., son of J.M. and Fannie Collier, 25 Oct 1898 – 12 Aug 1900
Collier, Rubie Joe, daughter of J.M. and Fannie Collier, 6 Mar 1903 – 1 Jul 1904
Cook, Angeline Maria Diorio, born 20 Oct 1915 at Pizzano, Italy – 8 Aug 1995; married 20 Aug 1939 in Chicago, Illinois; "They lived in Altoona, Alabama 1940 – 1995"
Cook, Cephas, died 1914; SS Joshua Cook
Cook, Charles, 1894 – 1942; SS Hettie Cook
Cook, Eliza J., 31 Mar 1865 – 18 Jun 1929; SS Issac S. Cook
Cook, Harley Eugene, born 19 Aug 1914 at Altoona – 2 Aug 1995; married 20 Aug 1939 in Chicago, Illinois; "They lived in Altoona, Alabama 1940 – 1995"
Cook, Hermon F., son of J.J. and M.L. Cook, 23 Mar 1911 – 9 Jul 1917
Cook, Hettie, 1892 – 1963; SS Charles Cook
Cook, Inez V., daughter of J.J. and M.L. Cook, 22 Oct 1913 – 10 Jun 1915
Cook, Issac S., 18 Sep 1863 – 12 Dec 1928; SS Eliza J. Cook
Cook, John Morris, 25 Aug 1931 – 21 May 1933
Cook, Joshua, died 1920; SS Cephas Cook
Cook, Lt. James A., 19 Nov 1923 – 19 Apr 1945
Cook, Ossie C., 1897 – 1944
Cooper, George L., 21 Dec 1892 – 25 Aug 1964; SS Mae H. Cooper
Cooper, Mae H., 22 Feb 1907 – 17 May 1971; SS George L. Cooper
Cooper, Minnie Ophelia, 1898 – 1935
Cooper, Oscar B., 3 May 1903 – 3 Jan 1974
Cooper, Robert B., 4 Nov 1926 – 8 Jul 1950, Alabama S2 USNR, WWII
Copeland, Alta Mae, 9 Mar 1917 – 29 Nov 1936
Copeland, Oscar, 27 May 1882 – 19 Nov 1947
Copeland, Osie, 19 Jun 1894 – 14 Sep 1969
Copeland, Robert, 31 Oct 1914 – 3 May 1983; US Navy
Couey, Anna Viola, 24 Oct 1892 – 28 Feb 1986; SS Frank Couey
Couey, Annie Jo, 13 Jan 1923 – 23 Jan 1991
Couey, Edd, 11 Jun 1892 – 11 Oct 1959
Couey, Erbie L., 5 Apr 1914 – 7 Mar 1971; Alabama, Sgt US Army, WWII
Couey, Frank, 22 Feb 1886 – 24 Jul 1955; SS Anna Viola Couey
Couey, Janet L., 23 Oct 1963 – 8 Feb 1990
Couey, Joseph Paul, 19 Jan 1920 – 27 Jun 1935
Couey, Mary, 6 Apr 1919 – 14 Jan 1989
Couey, Nobie C., 4 Aug 1890 – 19 Oct 1965
Couey, Patsy, 13 Jul 1956, [only date recorded; small homemade concrete monument]
Couey, Robert W., 18 Nov 1918 – 21 Jun 1981; Pvt US Army, WWII
Couey, Tommie L., 29 Nov 1926 – 22 Dec 1979; father; PFC US Army, Korea; SS Joyce D. Wood
Covey, Infant, [no dates recorded, surname may actually be "Couey"]
Cowan, Eulice D., 6 May 1923 – 29 Jan 1982; SS Gracie M. Cowan; married 23 Jun 1948
Cowan, Gracie M., 14 Mar 1930 – 17 Jan 1996; SS Eulice D. Cowan; married 23 Jun 1948
Cowart, Lois, 6 Dec 1899 – 22 Mar 1902
Cox, Jonathan M., 19 Aug 1941 – 22 Dec 1973
Cox, Mary Ola, 22 Feb 1919 – 14 Jul 1983; SS William Morris Cox
Cox, William Morris, 21 Aug 1915 – 16 Jul 1982; SS Mary Ola Cox
Crocker, William G., 16 Apr 1889 – 5 Aug 1956; Alabama, Pvt US Army, WWI
Crockett, Infants, of Mr. and Mrs. Arthur Crockett, [no dates recorded]
Crump, David Hanby, 1873 – 1929

Crump, Era Reavis, 1885 – 1919
Crump, Infant, of Mr. and Mrs. D.H. Crump, 17 Feb 1908 – 3 Mar 1908
Cummings, 16 Jun 1908 – 1 Jan 1956
Dabbs, Evelyn E., 26 May 1916 – 14 Jul 1917
Dabbs, Fannie S., 20 May 1890 – 15 Mar 1983
Dabbs, Reuben H., 28 Nov 1877 – 27 Sep 1961
Davenport, Agnes M., 25 Aug 1904 – 28 Nov 1992; SS Herbert W. Davenport
Davenport, Alton, 8 Apr 1905 – 28 Jan 1976; SS Minor Lee Davenport
Davenport, Billie S., 2 Jan 1931 – 21 Apr 1998; SS Joseph D. Davenport
Davenport, Bobby F., Jr., born and died 24 Oct 1966
Davenport, C.W. "Slick," 16 Apr 1926 – [rest of date missing]; SS Velma R. Davenport; married 9 Dec 1950
Davenport, Clarence, 9 Nov 1914 – 16 Nov 1979; SS Mae Ottis Davenport
Davenport, D. Newt, 28 Mar 1888 – 24 Feb 1965; SS Fannie D. Davenport
Davenport, Ed, 15 Mar 1899 – 11 Nov 1969; SS Shelta M. Davenport
Davenport, Edna K., 12 Jul 1921 – [rest of date missing]; SS Hershel E. Davenport
Davenport, Fannie D., 5 Jul 1895 – 25 Feb 1989; SS D. Newt Davenport
Davenport, Grover, 27 Jul 1892 – 13 Apr 1973; SS Roxie Davenport
Davenport, Herbert W., 8 Apr 1901 – 13 Apr 1972; SS Agnes M. Davenport
Davenport, Hershel E., 32 Nov 1921 – [rest of date missing]; SS Edna K. Davenport
Davenport, Howard D., 8 Jun 1933 – 8 Sep 1933
Davenport, James H., 29 Dec 1924 – 8 Dec 2000; US Navy, WWII; SS Sadie H. Davenport
Davenport, James Larry, 27 Sep 1947 – 13 Feb 1957
Davenport, Joseph D., 17 Dec 1923 – 24 May 1989; S1 US Navy, WWII; SS Billy S. Davenport
Davenport, Mae Ottis, 18 Aug 1919 – [rest of date missing]; SS Clarence Davenport
Davenport, Margaret L. "Jack," 4 Oct 1917 – 19 Sep 1987; SS Thomas "Chuck" Davenport
Davenport, Mildred F., 6 Sep 1928 – 23 Feb 1930
Davenport, Minor Lee, 25 Jul 1908 – [rest of date missing]; SS Alton Davenport
Davenport, Myrtle Ann, 31 Jul 1936 – 27 May 1955
Davenport, Ralph, 31 Jan 1919 – 5 Apr 1992; CCS US Navy, WWII
Davenport, Raymond Douglas, 19 May 1941 – 8 Jan 1976
Davenport, Roxie, 17 Jul 1901 – 19 Mar 1983; SS Grover Davenport
Davenport, Ruby Farley, 13 Jul 1935 – [rest of date missing]; SS Vernon Eugene "Henry" Davenport; married 27 Mar 1957
Davenport, Sadie H., 31 Jan 1940 – [rest of date missing]; SS James H. Davenport
Davenport, Shelta M., 21 Apr 1905 – 17 Sep 1981; SS Ed Davenport
Davenport, Susan, 8 Dec 1959 – 8 Dec 1959
Davenport, Thomas "Chuck," 10 Aug 1908 – 12 May 1987; SS Margaret L. "Jack" Davenport
Davenport, Velma R., 27 May 1928 – 24 Aug 1992; SS C.W. "Slick" Davenport; married 9 Dec 1950
Davenport, Vernon Eugene "Henry," 16 May 1932 – 16 Apr 1991; SS Ruby Farley Davenport; married 27 Mar 1957
Davidson, Charles O., [infant; no dates recorded]
Davidson, Eddie Odis, 23 Jul 1912 – 19 Jan 1931
Davidson, Lother Harwell, 15 Feb 1910 – 4 Mar 1988; Tec 4 US Army, WWII
Davidson, Maude C., 7 Mar 1910 – 4 Sep 1989; SS Sessel H. Davidson
Davidson, Minnie Nora, 1 Mar 1883 – 3 Nov 1954
Davidson, Newt H., 22 May 1879 – 1 Sep 1925
Davidson, Sessel H., 30 Nov 1907 – 11 Nov 1985; SS Maude C. Davidson
Davis, Cecil H., 1917 – 1984; SS Margie T. Davis
Davis, Margie T., 1922 – 1973; SS Cecil H. Davis
Deerman, Ferrell Eugene, 22 Mar 1896 – 9 Oct 1980; SS Ona Mae Deerman
Deerman, James Edwin, 26 Jun 1928 – 31 Mar 1996; Sgt US Army, WWII
Deerman, Ona Mae, 13 Oct 1898 – 25 Oct 1986; SS Ferrell Eugene Deerman
DeLoach, Thomas Earl, 19 Sep 1908 – 24 Dec 1990
DeLoach, Thomas H., 4 Jun 1942 – 25 Jan 1999
Denson, Ira McCain, 3 Mar 1895 – 19 Jan 1966; SS J.M. Denson
Denson, J.M., 1 Jun 1889 – 24 Jun 1966; SS Ira McCain Denson
Dickerson, Robert L., son of J. and E. Dickerson, 17 Nov 1884 – 21 Feb 1896
Dill, James F., 19 Dec 1898 – 31 Jan 1986; SS Rosa Pearl Dill
Dill, Rosa Pearl, 13 Sep 1907 – 22 Nov 1984; SS James F. Dill
Dillard, Annie W., 26 Feb 1909 – 19 May 1999; SS Sam Dillard

Dillard, Delia F., 26 Jun 1893 – 20 Jan 1979; SS Luther D. Dillard
Dillard, James Alton, 16 Sep 1934 – 30 Jan 1972
Dillard, Lloyd B., 21 May 1916 – 11 Jun 1957
Dillard, Luther D., 9 Sep 1892 – 13 Oct 1973; SS Delia F. Dillard
Dillard, Sam, 31 Mar 1907 – 13 May 1975; SS Annie W. Dillard
Dixon, Alvin Earl, 1 Jan 1921 – 18 Jul 1973; SS E. Evelyn Dixon
Dixon, E. Evelyn, 4 Jul 1925 – 21 Nov 1992; SS Alvin Earl Dixon
Dobbins, Berta B., 1896 – 1966; SS Richard Dickie Dobbins
Dobbins, John, died 27 Apr 1918, aged 65 years
Dobbins, Kathleen, 27 Apr 1921 – 26 Aug 1930
Dobbins, Mary Ellen, 25 Nov 1854 – 12 Sep 1909
Dobbins, Nellie, daughter or R. and Bertie Dobbins, 30 Jan 1916 – 10 Aug 1917
Dobbins, Richard Dickie, 1884 – 1952; SS Berta B. Dobbins
Dobbins, Richard, Jan 1852 – 19 Jul 1915
Dodd, Diane F., 29 Jul 1952 – 24 Dec 1999; SS Kenneth D. Dodd
Dodd, John Marion, son of Mr. and Mrs. R.A. Dodd, 20 Apr 1913 – 31 Oct 1917
Dodd, Kenneth D., 29 Sep 1957 – [rest of date missing]; SS Diane F. Dodd
Dorman, Addie A., 30 Jan 1844 – [rest of date never inscribed]; SS Jesse C. Dorman
Dorman, Jesse C., 23 Jul 1837 – 12 Jul 1920; SS Addie A. Dorman
Dorsey, E.C., died 27 Mar 1904
Dorsey, E.E., died 5 Apr 1902
Dorsey, Emma, died 27 Mar 1904
Dorsey, Florence C., 13 Nov 1899 – 8 Mar 1968
Dorsey, J.W., died 19 May 1904
Dorsey, James C., 3 Sep 1889 – 1 Aug 1964; Alabama 2d Lt Co A 52 Infantry, WWI
Dorsey, Mildred, died 28 Apr 1905
Dorsey, S.E., died 13 Oct 1907
Dover, Forest L., 12 Jul 1885 – 17 Nov 1914; Masonic emblem
Dover, James, 6 Oct 1865 – 29 Oct 1943; SS Mary Dover
Dover, Mary, 16 May 1865 – 22 Oct 1943; SS James Dover
Dover, Sarah A., Nov 1854 – 18 Sep 1930; SS William F. Dover
Dover, William F., 2 Jun 1862 – 21 Feb 1941; SS Sarah A. Dover
Dowling, Frances M. Robbins, wife of Thomas F. Dowling, 9 Mar 1880 – 28 Mar 1912
Dowling, Myrtle E. Ross, 16 Nov 1914 – 23 Oct 1985; SS Thomas Francis Dowling II
Dowling, Thomas Francis, II, 20 Mar 1912 – 12 Apr 1986; SS Myrtle E. Ross
Drake, Leonard, 18 May 1895 – 18 Dec 1915
Drake, Susie, wife of S.E. Drake, 22 Mar 1863 – 6 Dec 1915
Dunn, Dewey, 24 Feb 1904 – 16 Jun 1983; SS Marie Dunn
Dunn, Marie, 25 Apr 1903 – 31 Jan 1994; SS Dewey Dunn
Durham, A.J., born in South Carolina 1818 – 1894
Edge, Hortense, 1870 – 1948
Edge, Julian, 1903 – 1922
Edge, W.H., 1874 – 1937
Edwards, Raymond Henry, 4 Mar 1908 – 24 Mar 1990; US Army WWII
Eller, Ardieth L., 19 Oct 1927 – 7 Oct 1999; SS Dennis L. Eller
Eller, Dennis L., 21 Jun 1909 – 20 Jun 1975; SS Ardieth L. Eller
Elliott, William T., 25 Feb 1861 – 22 Dec 1913
Ellis, W.C., 5 Jun 1911 – 7 Nov 1995; SS Willis J. Ellis
Ellis, Willis J., 27 May 1913 – 12 Jan 1981; SS W.C. Ellis
Ellison, B.H., 24 Jan 1854 – 24 Aug 1933, [B.H. Ellison married Lila C. Dickerson 3 Dec 1874, Blount County]
Ellison, Carl, 31 Jan 1932 – 12 Mar 1993
Ellison, Charles, 15 Jan 1942 – [rest of date missing]; SS Dorothy M. Ellison
Ellison, Clarence E., 3 Dec 1905 – 25 Aug 1985; SS Girdie Ellison
Ellison, Clifford D., 28 Oct 1915 – 9 May 1994; SS Glodis C. Ellison; married 25 May 1935
Ellison, Deborah Lee Towe, 3 Oct 1958 – 15 Jan 2000
Ellison, Dorothy M., 15 Aug 1940 – 22 Sep 1970; SS Charles Ellison
Ellison, John H., Dr., 13 Apr 1862 – 26 Sep 1917; SS Fannie E. Ellison
Ellison, Elsie Bynum, 6 Jun 1891 – 20 Feb 1986; SS Herbert Ellison

Ellison, Eunice Arnold, 22 Oct 1880 – 7 Jul 1954; SS Webster J. Ellison
Ellison, Fannie E., 13 Sep 1868 – 13 Feb 1939; SS Dr. John H. Ellison
Ellison, Girdie, 24 Apr 1908 – 1 Dec 1987; SS Clarence E. Ellison
Ellison, Glodis C., 5 Feb 1920 – [rest of date missing]; SS Clifford D. Ellison; married 25 May 1935
Ellison, Henry Garlington, son of Dr. J.H. and F.E. Ellison, 30 Apr 1897 – 16 Oct 1901
Ellison, Herbert, 1890 – 1929; SS Elsie Bynum Ellison
Ellison, Holden Fowler, 20 Mar 1913 – 21 Sep 1986; SS Madge Moore Ellison
Ellison, Infant, son of W.J. and Eunice Ellison, born and died 7 Oct 1915
Ellison, L.C., wife of B.H. Ellison, 7 Mar 1857 – 7 Sep 1923, [Lila C. Dickerson married B.H. Ellison 3 Dec 1874, Blount County]
Ellison, Louis William, 9 Jan 1869 – 15 May 1952; SS Nettie Phillips Ellison
Ellison, Madge Moore, 4 Sep 1918 – 22 Sep 1975; SS Holden Fowler Ellison
Ellison, Mintora, 30 Nov 1874 – 5 Jul 1958
Ellison, Mrs. A.B. Nelson, wife of W.L. Ellison, 23 Sep 1850 – 15 Nov 1911
Ellison, Nettie Phillips, 16 Sep 1872 – 24 Sep 1966; SS Louis William Ellison
Ellison, Ottis Turner, 30 Mar 1910 – 13 Jul 1969; SS Tinnie Lee Ellison
Ellison, Ruth S., daughter of H.B. and Mollie Ellison, 5 Jul 1897 – 23 May 1936
Ellison, Tinnie Lee, 20 Feb 1915 – 15 Mar 1990; SS Ottis Turner Ellison
Ellison, Webster J., 7 Feb 1879 – 4 Apr 1968; SS Eunice Arnold Ellison
Farmer, Christine, 18 Mar 1928 – 10 Sep 2002; SS J.T. Farmer; married 15 Feb 1946
Farmer, J.T., 8 Oct 1926 – 13 May 1990; MM3 US Navy; SS Christine Farmer; married 15 Feb 1946
Farmer, Pearl C., 23 Nov 1905 – 28 Jan 1967
Fendley, [surname carved on rock, first name unreadable]
Fendley, Sarah A., 12 Oct 1820 – 11 May 1920, [a newer monument has replaced what seemed to be an original hand carved monument; Sarah was widow of William Fendley, a Private in Company G of the 7th Georgia Infantry, CSA; Alabama Confederate Pension Applications]
Ferguson, Willie, 15 Jun 1874 – 23 Dec 1938
Fluharty, Charlotte W., 23 May 1950 – 12 May 1980
Fluharty, Lessie Brown, 19 May 1925 – [rest of date missing]; SS Richard D. Fluharty
Fluharty, Richard D., 15 Jan 1916 – 20 Apr 1996; Cpl US Army, WWII; SS Lessie Brown Fluharty
Ford, Duglas M., 14 Aug 1928 – 8 Feb 1984; SS Martha B. Ford
Ford, Martha B., 14 Jan 1934 – 11 Feb 1976; SS Duglas M. Ford
Fore, Inez H., 6 May 1926 – [rest of date missing]; SS John F. Fore
Fore, John F., 16 Dec 1921 – 19 Jul 1992; SS Inez H. Fore
Forney, Mildred E. Peeples, 20 Oct 1912 – 13 Feb 2000
Foster, James Ellie, 14 Nov 1913 – 5 Jun 1973; SS Mary Lurene Foster
Foster, Louie E., 25 Nov 1909 – 15 May 1961; Alabama, PFC Co B 751 Tank Bn
Foster, Mary Lurene, 23 Nov 1914 – 27 Jun 1997; SS James Ellie Foster
Fowler, Alma S., 28 Oct 1897 – 9 Oct 1984; SS Elmer E. Fowler
Fowler, Elmer E., 9 Nov 1895 – 5 Apr 1979; SS Alma S. Fowler
Franklin, J.L., 5 Sep 1937 – 4 Nov 1998; SSg US Army, Vietnam
Franklin, Jamie Inez, 25 Oct 1922 – 25 Jan 1971; SS Perry Clyde Franklin
Franklin, John Marvin, 1914 – 1943
Franklin, Perry Clyde, 14 Apr 1919 – 22 Sep 1979; PFC US Army, WWII; SS Jamie Inez Franklin
Freeman, C.M., 17 Jan 1899 – 18 Oct 1979; SS C.M. Freeman
Freeman, Dora G., 17 Dec 1882 – 1 Apr 1980; SS Zach J. Freeman
Freeman, Eldora F., 5 Nov 1908 – 26 Oct 1996; SS C.M. Freeman
Freeman, Faye Nell, 5 Dec 1931 – 5 Apr 1934
Freeman, Irene, 17 Sep 1903 – 14 Mar 1935
Freeman, Paul A., 1 May 1910 – 27 Apr 1978; US Army, WWII
Freeman, Twins, sons of Irene and Cliff Freeman, Jan 1927, [only date recorded]
Freeman, Zach J., 2 Oct 1882 – 16 May 1956; SS Dora G. Freeman
Frix, Camilla, daughter of C.R. and F.M. Frix, 11 Sep 1902 – 21 Sep 1904
Frix, J.J., 20 Sep 1853 – 30 Dec 1922
Frix, M.C., wife of J.J. Frix, 25 Dec 1854 – 3 Sep 1924
Gaither, Elzora M., 11 Mar 1928 – [rest of date missing]; SS James Parks Gaither
Gaither, James Parks, 7 May 1920 – 11 Jan 1975; SS Elzora M. Gaither
Gash, Della, 7 Aug 1880 – 20 Aug 1959; SS W.R. Gash
Gash, Thomas B., 1868 – 1943

Gash, W.R., 4 Aug 1873 – 11 Nov 1940; SS Della Gash
George, J.C., 6 Nov 1934 – 26 Feb 1935
Gibbs, Clarice J. Patterson, 23 Dec 1937 – 11 Oct 1995; SS John Marshall Gibbs; married 27 Jun 1958
Gibbs, Corinne Turner, 9 Sep 1905 – 26 Jun 1961; SS Henry Lester Gibbs
Gibbs, David Arthur, 16 Jul 1963 – [rest of date missing]; son, SS James Ellis and Selma Turner Gibbs
Gibbs, Flossie L., 15 Nov 1909 – [rest of date missing]; SS Herman O. Gibbs
Gibbs, Henry Lester, 3 Jul 1906 – 28 Sep 1960; SS Corinne Turner Gibbs
Gibbs, Herman O., 17 Jul 1906 – 10 Mar 1979; SS Flossie L. Gibbs
Gibbs, James Ellis, 7 Oct 1923 – 28 Jun 2001; father, SS David Arthur and Selma Turner Gibbs
Gibbs, John Marshall, 20 Jun 1926 – [rest of date missing]; SS Clarice J. Patterson Gibbs, married 27 Jun 1958
Gibbs, Mae Stanfield, 8 May 1906 – 25 Dec 1998
Gibbs, Selma Turner, 27 Apr 1933 – [rest of date missing]; mother, SS David Arthur and James Ellis Gibbs
Gibson, James, 23 Nov 1884 – 28 Jan 1919
Gilley, Johnny, [no dates recorded]
Gilliland, Dentice, 21 Oct 1930 – [rest of date missing]; SS Glenda Gilliland
Gilliland, Glenda, 4 May 1939 – [rest of date missing]; SS Dentice Gilliland
Godbey, John Marshell, 4 Nov 1929 – 6 Feb 1932
Goforth, Amanda A., 31 Mar 1861 – 27 Feb 1926; SS J.T. Goforth [two monuments: older one reads "Mandy A. wife of J.T. Goforth"]
Goforth, J.T., 3 Feb 1851 – 19 Sep 1929; SS Amanda A. Goforth
Gravitt, Janie Thompson, 13 Nov 1886 – 28 Apr 1973
Green, Elbert A., 17 Jun 1916 – 10 Mar 1975; SS Flora Mae Green
Green, Flora Mae, 29 May 1910 – 8 Apr 1995; SS Elbert A. Green
Greer, Bessie Lee, wife of Earnest A. Greer, 29 Dec 1897 – 8 Apr 1926
Greer, Ernest A., 18 Feb 1887 – 29 Jun 1952
Griffin, Pearl B., 29 Jun 1908 – 25 Apr 1976; SS Robert M. Griffin
Griffin, Robert M., 17 Jan 1921 – [rest of date missing]; SS Pearl B. Griffin
Gunter, Dewey, 13 Sep 1899 – 9 Dec 1984; SS Pearl D. Gunter
Gunter, Lora, 25 Oct 1895 – 14 Apr 1919
Gunter, N Avery D., 21 Feb 1915 – 25 Dec 1990; SS Roy D. Gunter; married 8 Feb 1946
Gunter, Pearl D., 8 Jun 1910 – 2 Aug 1991; SS Dewey Gunter
Gunter, Roy D., 23 Sep 1909 – 11 Jun 1992; SS N Avery D. Gunter; married 8 Feb 1946
Gunter, Sam, 18 Oct 1875 – 30 Jan 1914; SS Savanah Gunter
Gunter, Savanah, 15 Nov 1877 – 25 Aug 1974; SS Sam Gunter
Hammett, Dena D., 13 May 1929 – [rest of date missing]; SS Floyd E. Hammett
Hammett, Floyd E., 18 Jul 1930 – 8 Oct 1992; TSgt US Air Force, WWII, Korea; SS Dena D. Hammett
Hammett, John Franklin, 16 Mar 1872 – 9 May 1917
Hancock, Nettie, 18 Jun 1861 – 5 Feb 1943
Harden, John, 19 Sep 1894 – 12 Feb 1949; Alabama, Pvt 162 Depot Brig, WWI
Hardin, Eva Ellison, daughter of John Henry Ellison, wife of Clarence S. Hardin, 16 Oct 1890 – 2 Dec 1980
Hardin, Hezekiah, 1859 – 1941; SS Menearve Hardin
Hardin, Margaret Lee, 22 May 1928 – 30 Sep 1971; SS R.L. (Joe) Hardin
Hardin, Menearve, 1864 – 1939; SS Hezekiah Hardin
Hardin, R.L. (Joe), 8 May 1926 – 9 Aug 1985; SS Margaret Lee Hardin
Harmon, Geraldine Dillard, 11 Jan 1925 – 27 Jun 1992
Harris, Ada E., 1880 – 1930
Harris, Carolyn Arnold, 13 Sep 1931 – 31 Jul 1989
Harris, Infant, daughter of Mr. and Mrs. Tully Harris, 1909, [only date recorded]
Harris, John S., 2 Jul 1934 – 14 May 1987
Harris, John W., 21 Dec 1911 – 5 Feb 1966; SS Verna F. Harris
Harris, Joseph B., 25 Nov 1860 – 19 Jul 1907
Harris, Lou Ella, 17 Jun 1872 – 8 Jul 1896
Harris, Seaborn, 1846 – 1936
Harris, Temperance, daughter of David Cowan, wife of W.A. Harris, 17 Apr 1839 – 25 Mar 1902, [Temperance C. Cowan married William A. Harris 11 Oct 1860, Blount County]
Harris, Tully, 1880 – 1931
Harris, Verna F., 11 Feb 1913 – [rest of date missing]; SS John W. Harris
Harris, W.A., 13 Oct 1839 – 6 Mar 1930, [William A. Harris married Temperance C. Cowan 11 Oct 1860, Blount County; Harris was a Private in Company C of the 12th Alabama Cavalry, CSA; 1907 Blount County Confederate Census, Microfilmed Confederate Service Records, and Alabama Confederate Pension Applications]

Hayes, Gloria Self, 27 Jan 1929 – 21 Oct 1973
Haynes, Talley W., 2 Oct 1926 – 23 Feb 1962
Helms, Billie Ray, son of Gene and Dortha Helms, 11 Aug 1950 – 12 Aug 1950
Helms, Larry E., 23 Dec 1943 – 28 Jan 1982; US Army, Vietnam, [another monument has the birth year 1931]
Hendricks, Annie G., 31 Jul 1892 – 19 Jul 1988
Hendricks, Ida Moseley, wife of John D. Hendricks, 19 Feb 1865 – 17 Jun 1929
Henegar, Cleveadell, 4 Jun 1911 – 5 Jan 2001
Henegar, Loyd H., 10 Mar 1909 – 27 Mar 1977
Henson, George W., 2 Mar 1897 – 19 Feb 1971
Henson, J.W., 18 Jan 1885 – 23 Mar 1914
Henson, Sarah L., 15 Aug 1866 – 2 Feb 1958
Henson, T.G., 19 Jun 1855 – 5 Jan 1918
Heptinstall, Christine "Christy," 6 Sep 1921 – 25 Feb 1983; SS David "Dee" Heptinstall; married 26 Oct 1940
Heptinstall, David "Dee," 24 Jan 1918 – [rest of date missing]; SS Christine "Christy" Heptinstall; married 26 Oct 1940
Heptinstall, J.C., 29 Jun 1860 – 12 Jul 1937; SS M.F. Heptinstall
Heptinstall, M.F., 4 May 1859 – 29 May 1936; SS J.C. Heptinstall
Heptinstall, Mallory D., 6 Oct 1888 – 2 Jun 1963; SS Pearl W. Heptinstall
Heptinstall, Pearl W., 9 Jun 1890 – 12 Feb 1972; SS Mallory D. Heptinstall
Herring, E.A., wife of J.M. Herring, 25 Nov 1837 – 1 Jan 1908
Herring, James M., 9 Jun 1823 – 15 Jul 1912
Higdon, Eudessa Culbert, 28 May 1908 – 25 May 2000; SS Samuel Randall Higdon; "Beloved school teacher for over 40 years"
Higdon, Samuel Randall, 14 Feb 1893 – 26 Feb 1972; WWI; SS Eudessa Culbert Higdon
Hilburn, Arretta V., 18 Feb 1921 – 12 Nov 1996; SS Edgar Marlo Hilburn
Hilburn, Edgar Marlo, 29 Mar 1919 – 18 Mar 1980; S1 US Navy, WWII; SS Arretta V. Hilburn
Hilburn, Gordon Chesteen, 22 Aug 1922 – 4 Feb 2002; PFC US Army Air Forces, WWII, Purple Heart; SS Sarah Aline Hilburn; married 8 Jul 1946
Hilburn, Herbert R., 17 May 1899 – 5 Mar 1974; SS Millie G. Hilburn
Hilburn, John Riley, Jr., 20 Dec 1978 – 9 Oct 1995, "Son of John Riley, Sr., great grandson of Herbert Riley"
Hilburn, Millie G., 17 Nov 1898 – 30 Jan 1967; SS Herbert R. Hilburn
Hilburn, Sarah Aline, 16 Mar 1929 – 12 Jul 1998; SS Gordon C. Hilburn; married 8 Jul 1946
Hill, Sue Cagle, 21 Jan 1930 – [rest of date missing]
Hobbs, Joseph J., Dec 1835 – Feb 1906; Private in Company E of the 30th Alabama Infantry, CSA
Hodges, Rufus M., 1866 – 1945; SS Sudie S. Hodges
Hodges, Sudie S., 1870 – 1954; SS Rufus M. Hodges
Holland, Bertha M., 11 Nov 1929 – [rest of date missing]; SS Oliver G. Holland
Holland, Oliver G., 25 Feb 1923 – 5 Jul 1978; SS Bertha M. Holland
Holmes, Ruby J. Walls, 21 Apr 1921 – 18 Aug 2000
Holtzclaw, Charles A., 1861 – 1938; SS Lula B. Holtzclaw
Holtzclaw, Cothran, son of Mr. and Mrs. C.A. Holtzclaw, 10 May 1915 – 10 Nov 1915
Holtzclaw, Infant, of Mr. and Mrs. H.L. Holtzclaw, born and died 25 Dec 1929
Holtzclaw, Lula B., 1874 – 1940; SS Charles A. Holtzclaw
Hopper, Arnell Ingram, 15 Jul 1922 – 19 Mar 2001; SS Wilber L. Hopper
Hopper, Christine Kelsoe, 10 Jan 1941 – [rest of date missing]; SS Raymond (Bud) Hopper
Hopper, Joan Melinda, 29 May 1954 – 30 May 1954
Hopper, Leon James, 15 Jun 1925 – 25 Aug 1984
Hopper, Minerva Octivia, 21 Apr 1949 – 22 Apr 1949
Hopper, Perry N., 23 Aug 1894 – 5 Jan 1972; SS Vinie L. Hopper
Hopper, Raymond (Bud), 4 Feb 1934 – 13 May 1995; PFC US Army, Korea; SS Christine Kelsoe Hopper
Hopper, Vinie L., 11 Apr 1895 – 9 Jul 1977; SS Perry N. Hopper
Hopper, Wilber L., 27 Mar 1918 – 14 Aug 1971; Alabama, Tec 4 Hq Sp Trps 6 Army, WWII
Horton, Cynthia E., wife of S.E. Horton, Oct 1839 – Feb 1915
Horton, Florence, daughter of J.R. and Eliza Horton, 7 Dec 1916 – 17 Sep 1917
Horton, James M., son of Rev. and Mrs. J.H. Horton, 30 Jun 1914 – 9 Jun 1916
Horton, James R., 1871 – 1958; SS Sarah E. Horton
Horton, Martha Fay Miles, 13 Nov 1908 – 13 Apr 1989; SS Walter Leon Horton
Horton, Paul T., son of I.H. and L.B. Horton, 22 Oct 1905 – 7 Oct 1906
Horton, Sarah E., 1875 – 1942; SS James R. Horton

Horton, Stephen E., 27 Mar 1845 – 1 Sep 1936, [Horton was a Private in Company H of the 38th Alabama Infantry, CSA; Alabama Confederate Pension Applications]
Horton, Walter Leon, 7 Mar 1915 – 2 Jun 1992; SS Martha Fay Miles Horton
House, Gerald E., 31 Aug 1932 – 25 Aug 1985; US Army, Korea
Hudson, Flora L., Nov 1922 – Nov 1926, [hand carved monument]
Humphries, Ann, 21 Feb 1897 – 11 Dec 1973; SS George Q. Humphries
Humphries, George Q., 13 Jul 1896 – 4 Jun 1971; SS Ann Humphries
Humphries, Hoyt, 25 Dec 1924 – 9 Jan 1944
Humphries, Odell Quincy, 26 May 1918 – 14 Aug 1971; US Marine
Hunt, Daniel, 11 Apr 1842 – 8 Oct 1912; SS Fredricka Hunt
Hunt, Fredricka, 29 Jan 1846 – 12 Jun 1931; SS Daniel Hunt
Huter, W.G., husband of Bertha Huter, 18 Jul 1884 – 11 Feb 1914
Huter, Willie C., son of W.G. and Bertha Huter, 5 Dec 1913 – 11 Jun 1916
Inman, John, 18 May 1826 – 29 Jul 1895, [broken monument]
Inman, Rhoda, 22 Jul 1857 – 10 Dec 1941
Inmon, Eugene, 2 Mar 1859 – 30 Mar 1926
Inmon, Jim, Oct 1860, age 42 years, [only date recorded]; SS Nancy J. Inmon
Inmon, Martha Jane, 19 Aug 1860 – 17 Nov 1947; SS Thomas Inmon
Inmon, Nancy J., 17 Aug 1861 – 27 Feb 1942; SS Jim Inmon
Inmon, Thomas, 2 Aug 1861 – 18 Sep 1937; SS Martha Jane Inmon
Inmon, Winnie, 17 Jul 1827 – 22 Jun 1910, [broken monument]
Isenhower, J.K. (Kitty), 1876 – 1949; SS Rev. E.J. Isenhower
Isenhower, E.J., Rev., 1876 – 1949; SS J.K. (Kitty) Isenhower
Jackson, E.I., 11 Jun 1890 – 9 Oct 1969; SS Mary Lee Jackson
Jackson, J.D., 19 Jan 1912 – 26 Aug 2002; SS Velma Jackson; married 2 Sep 1942
Jackson, Mary Lee, 24 Aug 1896 – 4 Jul 1960; SS E.I. Jackson
Jackson, O.Z., 3 Jan 1922 – 31 May 1990
Jackson, Velma, 6 Jan 1907 – 23 Mar 1996; SS J.D. Jackson; married 2 Sep 1942
Jenkins, Howard D., 27 Dec 1922 – [rest of date missing]; SS V. Loree Jenkins; married 14 Jan 1946
Jenkins, V. Loree, 10 Jul 1926 – [rest of date missing]; SS Howard D. Jenkins; married 14 Jan 1946
Jennings, Caroline, daughter of Alfred and Martha Reese, 21 Apr 1873 – 2 Dec 1891
Jennings, Elizabeth, 18 Oct 1826 – 21 Jan 1903
Jennings, John Robert, 11 Jan 1856 – 29 Aug 1894
Jennings, W.M., 6 Apr 1824 – 4 Feb 1905; SS Elizabeth Jennings
Johnson, C.J., 7 Apr 1920 – [rest of date missing]; Masonic emblem; SS Willie Mae Johnson
Johnson, Herman Lee, 19 Jul 1901 – 13 Aug 1982; SS Lula G. Johnson
Johnson, Jewell C., 24 Feb 1912 – 6 Feb 1996; SS Jones C. Johnson
Johnson, Jones C., 12 Oct 1907 – 13 Sep 1971; Alabama, S2 USNR, WWII; SS Jewell C. Johnson
Johnson, Lula G., 8 May 1902 – 26 Nov 1985; SS Herman Lee Johnson
Johnson, Sarah C., Mar 1844 – Oct 1922
Johnson, Willie Mae, 14 Oct 1919 – [rest of date missing]; SS C.J. Johnson
Johnston, Agnes, 16 Jul 1911 – 25 Sep 1995; SS James C. and Bonnie Johnston
Johnston, Annie, 1887 – 1948; SS Cephus Johnston
Johnston, Bonnie, 14 Jul 1931 – 2 Feb 1939; SS James C. and Agnes Johnston
Johnston, Cephus, 1888 – 1968; SS Annie Johnston
Johnston, Donald, 28 Nov 1929 – 23 Jun 1998; SS Myra Johnston
Johnston, James C., 25 Sep 1909 – 2 Nov 1981; S1 US Navy, WWII; SS Bonnie and Agnes Johnston
Johnston, Myra, 6 Feb 1928 – [rest of date missing]; SS Donald Johnston
Joiner, Earl, 2 Apr 1943 – 20 Mar 1997; SS Gloria Joiner; married 25 Apr 1965
Joiner, Gloria, 2 Mar 1947 – [rest of date missing]; SS Earl Joiner; married 25 Apr 1965
Jones, Clyde W., 10 Feb 1913 – 4 May 1976; SS Lillie H. Jones
Jones, Clyde, Jr., 1955 – 1988
Jones, Floyd E., 4 Feb 1910 – 2 Jul 1972
Jones, H.T., 25 Dec 1908 – 16 Jul 1990
Jones, Lewis Ellington, 1878 – 1917 "Author of *There is Power in the Blood, We Shall See the King Some Day,* and other songs"
Jones, Lillie H., 21 Sep 1933 – 24 Dec 1982; SS Clyde W. Jones
Jones, Mary F., 19 Feb 1893 – 22 Feb 1940
Jones, Mary Scott, 16 Dec 1879 – 3 Aug 1954
Jones, Ola V., 13 Dec 1925 – 15 Feb 1926

Jones, Ruby M., 8 May 1912 – [rest of date missing]
Jones, Shely E., 26 Nov 1890 – 20 Jun 1953
Jones, W. Lucille, 3 Jun 1915 – 29 Sep 1976
Kaufman, John A., son of C.A. and Gertrude Kaufman, 16 Sep 1912 – 1 Sep 1914
Kennedy, Delia Moore, 4 Mar 1907 – 1 Jan 1979
Kent, Belvie K., 22 Feb 1893 – 31 Jan 1918
Kent, Elmer L., 15 Feb 1915 – 3 Jul 1983; SS Nell Jo Kent
Kent, Grace, 31 Aug 1912 – 3 Feb 1978
Kent, Nell Jo, 8 Jun 1917 – 21 Jan 1991; SS Elmer L. Kent
Kent, Nora C., 13 Sep 1888 – 11 Sep 1969
Kent, Rastus R., 26 Mar 1880 – 19 Jun 1953
Kent, Ruby May, daughter of W.T. and Estell Kent, 6 Feb 1912 – 8 Sep 1914
Kerr, Annette Copeland, 8 Jul 1935 – 31 Oct 2001; SS James A. Kerr; married 6 Sep 1953
Kerr, James A., 26 Oct 1927 – [rest of date missing]; SS Annette Copeland Kerr; married 6 Sep 1953
Kidd, Buey Earnest, 3 Jul 1905 –23 Aug 1966; SS Kathleen Virginia Kidd
Kidd, Kathleen Virginia, 17 Feb 1917 – 29 Jan 1997; SS Buey Earnest Kidd
Kilgore, Gladys M., 28 Apr 1906 – 31 Mar 1937
Kilgore, Ralph T., 20 Sep 1927 – 30 Jan 1975; SSgt US Air Force
King, James Edward, 17 Jan 1926 – 15 Apr 1995; SMSgt US Air Force, WWII, Korea, Vietnam; SS Janet E. King
King, Janet E., 26 Jul 1950 – [rest of date missing]; SS James E. King
King, Lois M. Webb, 5 Jul 1904 – 15 Jun 1965
King, Martha Lamb, wife of T.M. King, 28 Feb 1845 – 24 Mar 1907, [Martha A. Lamb married Thomas M. King 17 Jan 1867, Blount County]
King, Ressa Belle, wife of Will D. King, 5 May 1886 – 24 Mar 1922
King, Thomas M., 25 Dec 1839 – 12 Jul 1911, [Thomas M. King married Martha A. Lamb 17 Jan 1867, Blount County; King was a Private in Company B of the 19th Alabama Infantry, CSA; 1907 Blount County Confederate Census and Microfilmed Confederate Service records]
King, V. Callie, 7 Oct 1875 – 17 Nov 1947
King, William D., 19 Sep 1882 – 7 Apr 1952; Masonic emblem
Kirk, Henry F., 16 May 1883 – 21 Jun 1969; SS Nancy F. Kirk
Kirk, Nancy F., 2 Mar 1885 – 20 May 1948; SS Henry F. Kirk
Knapp, Martha S., 24 Jan 1915 – 17 Jan 1995
Knox, Cora B., 17 Sep 1888 – 27 Jun 1957
Knox, Fred, 20 May 1913 – 16 Dec 1932
Knox, James E., 28 Sep 1915 – 24 Dec 1965
Knox, John W., 28 Aug 1876 – 28 Mar 1927
Knutt, Jewell M. Willis, 21 Jun 1919 – 20 Jul 1991
Lackey, Edgar W., 9 Jan 1913 – 24 Nov 1968; SS Mable L. Lackey
Lackey, Jamie Lee, 23 Sep 1955 – 24 Sep 1955
Lackey, Mable L., 4 Jul 1912 – 7 Sep 1986; SS Edgar W. Lackey
Lambert, Charles H., 5 Dec 1937 – 2 Feb 1938
Lancaster, Elsa E., 9 May 1951 – 11 Sep 1989
Larison, Sam, 25 Mar 1891 – 30 Jul 1949; Alabama, Pvt Mg Tng Center, WWI
Laughlin, Bobbie Lee, 6 Dec 1934 – [rest of date missing]; SS Talmadge Troy Laughlin
Laughlin, Charlie, 13 Mar 1903 – 3 Aug 1967; SS Hazel C. Laughlin
Laughlin, Hazel C., 7 Jul 1907 – 16 Oct 1989; SS Charlie Laughlin
Laughlin, Jerry Wayne, 5 Apr 1949 – 1 Apr 1992
Laughlin, Lila A., 20 Jul 1915 – 30 May 1989
Laughlin, Talmadge Troy, 4 Mar 1935 – 5 Nov 1987; PFC US Marine Corps; SS Bobbie Lee Laughlin
Laughlin–McBride, Voyne Sue, 13 Aug 1941 – 3 Mar 1997
Lee, Alfred A., 21 Mar 1922 – 3 Jun 1991
Lee, Frances M., 8 May 1861 – 10 Jan 1930; SS W.M. Lee
Lee, Luther Allen, 18 May 1889 – 3 Jan 1958; SS Mary Jane Lee
Lee, Mary Jane, 18 Jul 1892 – 30 Apr 1952; SS Luther Allen Lee
Lee, W.M., 12 Feb 1858 – 18 Dec 1923; SS Frances M. Lee
Letherwood, Arthur L., 13 May 1917 – 25 Dec 1993; Tec 4 US Army, WWII; SS Mable Ruth Ward Letherwood
Letherwood, Mable Ruth Ward, 20 Oct 1921 – 3 Dec 1996; SS Arthur L. Letherwood
Letherwood, Mona Rae, 16 Jul 1944 – 18 Jul 1944

Lewis, Celia "Stanfield," 28 Jul 1921 – 20 Jan 1999
Lewis, Charlene, born and died 20 Apr 1964
Lindsay, Enoch H., Jr., 1 May 1925 – 9 Dec 1971
Little, Bessie, 19 Feb 1933 – [rest of date missing]; SS Thaddeus Little
Little, Russell, 7 Jun 1958 – 27 Oct 1997
Little, Thaddeus, 7 Dec 1929 – 19 May 1984; SS Bessie Little
Loggins, Clara Louise, 3 Feb 1991, [only date recorded]
Loggins, Donald, 2 Nov 1943 – 2 Nov 1943 [two monuments]
Loggins, Harley Milton, 5 Oct 1920 – 21 Feb 1998
Loggins, William Woodrow, 1919 – 1979; PFC US Army, WWII
Lovell, Donald Aaron, 14 Oct 1953 – 18 Dec 1953
Lybrand, Clifton L., 24 Nov 1933 – 13 Sep 1976
Maddox, Emma Dillard Conn, 7 Sep 1867 – 29 Oct 1937
Mann, Barbara Ann, 7 Aug 1949 – 4 Aug 1964
Mann, Belmon, 1905 – 1988; SS Eula Mann
Mann, Charles C., 1870 – 1944; SS Ola Mann
Mann, Charley Gene, 22 Sep 1944 – 1 Jun 1945
Mann, Eula, 1910 – 1979; SS Belmon Mann
Mann, Floyd, 19 May 1916 – 26 May 1995
Mann, Gertrude, daughter of C.C. and Ola Mann, 14 Feb 1905 – 8 Feb 1930
Mann, Hoye Miller, 1 Sep 1906 – 7 May 1967; SS Roland Elbert Mann
Mann, Jessie C., 10 Apr 1920 – 7 May 1996
Mann, Michael Shay, 5 Dec 1976 – 5 Dec 1976
Mann, Ola, 1878 – 1953; SS Charles C. Mann
Mann, Roland Elbert, 3 Sep 1905 – 16 Dec 1985; SS Hoye Miller Mann
Mann, Rufus A., 9 Jun 1909 – 29 Jul 1975
Mann, Thomas, 19 Sep 1914 – 21 Jun 1958
Mason, Jacob Scott, 14 Nov 1993 – 24 Feb 2000; picture
Matthews, Mae K., 28 Dec 1923 – 2 Mar 1985
McAfee, Alvis James, 28 Jun 1921 – 9 Mar 1991; SS Juanita Phillips McAfee
McAfee, Juanita Phillips, 16 May 1922 – [rest of date missing]; SS Alvis James McAfee
McAuley, Carrie L., 12 Oct 1892 – 22 Feb 1965; SS Clyde McAuley
McAuley, Clyde, 28 May 1887 – 14 Sep 1974; Masonic emblem; SS Carrie L. McAuley
McAuley, Hartsworth, 25 Apr 1895 – 19 Jul 1946
McAuley, Lula S., 1856 – 1932; SS Thomas J. McAuley
McAuley, Thomas J., 1851 – 1927; SS Lula S. McAuley
McCay, J.D., 25 Jan 1879 – 17 Feb 1923; SS Ola B. McCay
McCay, Ola B., 17 Oct 1887 – 11 Jul 1979; SS J.D. McCay
McCourt, George B., 1 Apr 1864 – 11 Jan 1942
McCourt, Mary, wife of George B. McCourt, 10 Aug 1857 – 13 Nov 1913
McCray, A. Clifton, 15 Jun 1906 – 5 Dec 1989; SS Flaucie L. McCray
McCray, Bessie L., 13 Jun 1898 – 12 Oct 1981; SS Klines W. McCray
McCray, Flaucie L., 25 Apr 1905 – 2 Oct 1989; SS A. Clifton McCray
McCray, Joe D. "Toots," 6 Jan 1937 – 14 Oct 1997
McCray, Klines W., 16 Mar 1895 – 18 Mar 1970; SS Bessie L. McCray
McCullers, Ethel, 14 May 1899 – 7 Apr 1980; SS Fred McCullers
McCullers, Fred, 8 Jul 1900 – 17 Feb 1964; SS Ethel McCullers
McCurry, Celesta, 28 May 1833 – 11 Nov 1912
McDade, George Washington, 20 Dec 1838 – 18 Apr 1908, [McDade was a Private in Company A of the 13th Alabama Cavalry, CSA; 1907 Blount County Confederate Census and Alabama Confederate Pension Applications]
McDade, Mrs. S.E., 25 Mar 1839 – 10 Sep 1906
McDaniel, Delia B., 16 Sep 1906 – 10 Jun 1997; SS Thomas D. McDaniel
McDaniel, Randy Lenn, 4 Aug 1961 – 23 Dec 1961
McDaniel, Robert Arthur, 2 Apr 1931 – 23 Apr 1948; picture
McDaniel, Thomas D., 11 Sep 1900 – 10 Dec 1958; SS Delia B. McDaniel
McDonough, Imogene Spurling, 15 Mar 1932 – 6 Oct 1992
McGlaughn, Jessie J., 24 Aug 1917 – 30 May 1982; SS Lucile McGlaughn
McGlaughn, Lucile, 12 Oct 1912 – [rest of date missing]; SS Jessie J. McGlaughn
McIlquham, Alice E., 1868 – 1932

McIlquhan, Arch, son of Andrew and Mary McIlquhan, 16 Apr 1886 – 19 Dec 1910
McMunn, Glenn, Dr., 26 Sep 1910 – 20 Nov 1999; SS Opal C. McMunn
McMunn, Opal C., 20 Dec 1919 – [rest of date missing]; SS Dr. Glenn McMunn
McNair, Helen W., 10 Feb 1939 – 7 May 1995; SS Roy A. McNair
McNair, Roy A., 7 Feb 1936 – 2 Mar 1971; SS Helen W. McNair
Mewbourn, John M., 17 Dec 1868 – 26 Oct 1954; SS Martha Mewbourn
Mewbourn, Martha, 1 Mar 1870 – 20 Jun 1949; SS John M. Mewbourn
Meyers, Bennie Winefield, 12 Dec 1933 – 9 Jul 1990
Meyers, Sally Marie, 16 Jul 1963 – 4 Feb 1989
Meyers, Stoney Burk, 14 Jul 1964 – 3 May 1996
Miller, Glenda M., 22 Mar 1943 – [rest of date missing]; SS Harold T. Miller; married 5 May 1971
Miller, Harold T., 22 May 1937 – 11 Jan 1999; SS Glenda M. Miller; married 5 May 1971
Miller, Jay V., 18 Aug 1915 – 10 Aug 1987
Miller, Martha Lula, 23 Aug 1871 – 30 Oct 1956; SS Robert Henry Miller, [Martha Lee married Robert H. Miller 8 Dec 1889, Blount County]
Miller, Robert Henry, 26 Feb 1865 – 25 Jun 1957; SS Martha Lula Miller, [Robert H. Miller married Martha Lee 8 Dec 1889, Blount County]
Miller, Thomas A., son of P.F. and Bessie Miller, 28 Jul 1915 – 15 Sep 1920
Mitchell, Daughter, of W.E. and V.E. Mitchell, 20 Dec 1904 – 23 Feb 1910
Mitchell, Milton E., 1 Jan 1914 – 13 Aug 1978; SS Sarah L. Mitchell
Mitchell, Sarah L., 6 Nov 1922 – 6 Jul 1990; SS Milton E. Mitchell
Mohon, Bobby, 1 Aug 1896 – 19 Jun 1974; SS Myrtle Miller Mohon
Mohon, Myrtle Miller, 30 May 1903 – 24 May 1988; SS Bobby Mohon
Moman, Porter Lee, son of Rev. A.C. and H.M. Moman, 1 Jan 1910 – 11 Jul 1911
Moody, Cheryl Rene, 11 Oct 1958 – 14 Oct 1958
Moody, Howard E., 14 Aug 1936 – 4 Oct 1990
Moore, Billy M., 20 Feb 1935 – 31 Jan 1998; SSgt US Air Force, Vietnam
Moore, Edna Carol, 29 Jun 1949 – 14 Dec 2000; SS Larry W. Moore; married 29 Sep 1967
Moore, Florence S., 11 Nov 1879 – 4 Jan 1944
Moore, Grady William, 31 Aug 1917 – 9 Dec 1972
Moore, James A., 3 May 1879 – 13 Jun 1946; SS Mattie L. Moore
Moore, James Rufus, 16 Jun 1858 – 16 Jan 1932
Moore, Larry W., 1 Jan 1949 – [rest of date missing]; SS Edna Carol Moore; married 29 Sep 1967
Moore, Mattie L., 22 Jul 1886 – [death date never inscribed]; SS James A. Moore
Moore, Nancy Lee Holmes, 30 May 1938 – [rest of date missing]; SS Robert Allen Moore; married 20 Apr 1957
Moore, Nathan W., son of J.A. and M.E. Moore, 15 Apr 1915 – 24 Dec 1927
Moore, Ora Belle, 3 Aug 1917 – 1 Jan 1992; SS Rufus Benjamin Moore
Moore, Robert Allen, 13 Jan 1936 – 21 Dec 1999; Masonic emblem; SS Nancy Lee Holmes; married 20 Apr 1957
Moore, Rufus Benjamin, 6 Sep 1915 – 10 Nov 1981; SS Ora Belle Moore
Moore, Sybil, 4 Aug 1931 – 9 Nov 1996
Morgan, Albert Clark, 24 Apr 1920 – 28 Mar 1994
Morgan, Anna Louella, 8 Aug 1880 – 21 Sep 1965; SS Charles Lee Morgan, Sr.
Morgan, Boston C., 28 Apr 1900 – 7 Nov 1931; SS Ila Mae Beaver Morgan
Morgan, C.L., 20 Apr 1916 – 28 May 1938; SS Lena Morgan
Morgan, Charles Lee, Sr., 27 Nov 1870 – 16 Feb 1952; SS Anna Louella Morgan
Morgan, Ila Mae Beaver, 15 Jun 1902 – 22 Jun 1935; SS Boston C. Morgan
Morgan, James Campbell, 11 Jan 1944 – 21 Nov 1986
Morgan, Jane Josephine, 9 Nov 1952 – 14 Jun 1986
Morgan, Jerry Max, 10 Jul 1936 – 11 Feb 1998
Morgan, John E., 1 Jul 1894 – 12 Mar 1967; SS Lonnie Mae Morgan
Morgan, Lena, 2 Nov 1898 – 22 Feb 1942; SS C.L. Morgan
Morgan, Lonnie Mae, 18 Sep 1909 – 30 Sep 1994; SS John E. Morgan
Morgan, Mary Nell Nelson, 1 Oct 1926 – 18 Aug 1988
Morgan, Minnie Toy, 27 Mar 1911 – [rest of date missing]; SS Oscar Underwood Morgan
Morgan, Oscar Underwood, 7 Jan 1914 – 19 Feb 1991; SS Minnie Toy Morgan
Morgan, Pearle, 7 Aug 1907 – 3 May 1992
Morris, W.F., 15 Jun 1860 – 8 Feb 1906
Morrison, John Bruce, 25 Nov 1893 – 28 May 1972; SS Lucille White Morrison

Morrison, Lucille White, 26 Oct 1906 – 1 Jul 1995; SS John Bruce Morrison
Morton, Nola Jane, 17 May 1909 – 19 Jul 1994; SS William Luther Morton; married 30 Dec 1924
Morton, Vanessa K., 14 Oct 1958 – 20 Dec 1961
Morton, William Luther, 9 Feb 1906 – 1 Jul 1969; SS Nola Jane Morton; married 30 Dec 1924
Moseley, Mrs. S.J., 23 May 1839 – 24 Sep 1925
Murphree, Alice Loretta, 26 Jan 1914 – 13 Dec 1990; SS Jewel McKinley Murphree
Murphree, Emma Thompson, 3 Jan 1918 – 26 Jul 1997
Murphree, Jewel McKinley, 20 Nov 1906 – 15 Jan 1980; SS Alice Loretta Murphree
Murphree, John Rankin, 10 Jan 1935 – 15 Nov 1987
Murphree, Morris Ray, 30 Jul 1943 – 16 Jul 1980
Murphree, Randall Edison, 11 Aug 1917 – 29 Jan 1988
Neely, Alfred T., 4 Oct 1902 – 5 Jun 1966; SS Ruby Sue Neely
Neely, Jerline Laughlin, 23 Dec 1931 – 16 Jan 1984
Neely, Ruby Sue, 23 Sep 1913 – 14 Mar 1982; SS Alfred T. Neely
Nelson, Agnes, daughter of A.S. and Inez Nelson, 22 Apr 1900 – 29 Sep 1900
Nelson, Albert Sidney, 1874 – 1938; SS Fannie Summers Nelson
Nelson, Annie E., 23 Feb 1885 – 2 Sep 1963; SS Thomas A. Nelson
Nelson, Fannie Summers, 29 Dec 1878 – 12 Apr 1968; SS Albert Sidney Nelson
Nelson, Felicia Bello, 1 Sep 1919 – 31 Aug 1991; SS T.A. Nelson
Nelson, Inez Murphree, wife of A.S. Nelson, 10 Dec 1875 – 22 Feb 1901
Nelson, Infant, daughter of A.S. and Fannie Nelson, 27 Feb 1911, [only date recorded]
Nelson, Infant, son of A.S. and F.L. Nelson, born and died 22 Nov 1906
Nelson, Max S., 3 Aug 1922 – 20 Feb 1965; SS Ursula Eckermann Nelson
Nelson, Nellie, daughter of Mr. and Mrs. A.S. Nelson, 7 Jun 1919, [only date recorded]
Nelson, Ruth, daughter of A.S. and Fannie Nelson, 16 May 1915 – 9 Sep 1916
Nelson, T.A., 9 Jan 1914 – 30 Oct 1992; SS Felicia Bello Nelson
Nelson, T.M., 12 Jun 1842 – 2 Mar 1898
Nelson, Thomas A., 1876 – 1945
Nelson, Thomas A., 24 Dec 1876 – 3 May 1945; SS Annie E. Nelson
Nelson, Ursula Eckermann, 2 Aug 1929 – [rest of date missing]; SS Max S. Nelson
Nelson, Wilma Buddy, 23 Jun 1924 – 11 Sep 1927
Nichols, Duard Wiley, 2 May 1913 – 19 Feb 1994; SS Estelle Byrant Nichols
Nichols, Ellen, 29 Aug 1924 – [rest of date missing]; SS H.C. "Bob" Nichols
Nichols, Estelle Bryant, 29 Jan 1916 – [rest of date missing]; SS Duard Wiley Nichols
Nichols, Garvis K., 8 Mar 1915 – 7 Apr 1975; SS Opal L. Nichols
Nichols, H.C. "Bob," 13 Mar 1915 – 27 Sep 2002; Masonic emblem; SS Ellen Nichols
Nichols, John T., 26 Nov 1887 – 7 Apr 1970; SS Lillie B. Nichols
Nichols, John Timothy, 6 Jan 1971 – 10 May 1971
Nichols, Lillie B., 6 Dec 1892 – 14 Jul 1972; SS John T. Nichols
Nichols, Opal L., 16 Sep 1916 – 20 Apr 1991; SS Garvis K. Nichols
Nichols, Sanrda Frances, 7 Jul 1963 – 20 Oct 1963
Nichols, Wyatt, 4 Oct 1943 – 17 May 1959
Nix, Arthur S., 12 Jan 1902 – 27 Apr 1979; SS Verdie Nix
Nix, Effie, 2 Jan 1904 – 10 Jun 1996; SS Emmett Nix
Nix, Emmett, 18 Aug 1900 – 23 Feb 1970; SS Effie Nix
Nix, Etha, 7 Feb 1928 – 22 Apr 1990; SS Lucille Nix
Nix, Fannie, 13 Mar 1923, age 41 years, [only date recorded]
Nix, John D., 2 Jan 1871 – 22 Oct 1939
Nix, Kathryn, 25 Dec 1930 – [rest of date missing]
Nix, Lucille, 18 Jun 1932 – [rest of date missing]; SS Etha Nix
Nix, Minnie, daughter of J.D. and F.A. Nix, 29 Oct 1901 – 4 Aug 1902
Nix, Rubie, daughter of J.D. and F.A. Nix, 3 Nov 1899 – 5 Nov 1899
Nix, Verdie, 17 Sep 1910 – 28 May 1999; SS Arthur S. Nix
Noojin, Clifford E., 19 Oct 1908 – 5 Sep 1932
Noojin, Infant, daughter of Mr. and Mrs. C.E. Noojin, 5 Aug 1930 – 15 Sep 1930
Norris, Dean, 3 Jul 1928 – 4 Mar 1984
Norris, Leon L., 26 Jun 1926 – 4 Apr 1994
Norris, Robert C., 1 Jul 1930 – 9 Jan 1977

Norris, Verna F., 2 Nov 1902 – 24 Jan 1990; SS W.Z. "Bill" Norris
Norris, W.Z. "Bill," 15 Sep 1896 – 23 Feb 1962; SS Verna F. Norris
Oliver, David Lewis, 23 Oct 1965 – 20 Apr 1995; married Tammy 7 Dec 1990
Olson, Kenneth W., 12 Nov 1918 – 3 Apr 1993; RM3 US Navy, WWII; SS Louise H. Olson
Olson, Louise H., 28 Dec 1921 – 23 Nov 1971; SS Kenneth W. Olson
Orr, Fred R., 24 Aug 1909 – 10 Sep 1984; SS Geneva Casey Orr
Orr, Gary Wayne, 5 Aug 1948 – 11 Nov 1967
Orr, Geneva Casey, 27 Oct 1919 – 19 Feb 1986; SS Fred R. Orr
Osborne, Woodrow, 18 Sep 1924 – 22 Apr 1962
Parker, Alvin, 18 Dec 1936 – 13 Jan 1937
Parker, Bessie Self, 9 Aug 1893 – 6 Mar 1970; SS Issac C. Parker
Parker, Florence Lee, 4 Jul 1900 – 12 Sep 1975; SS Walter Frank Parker
Parker, Issac C., 22 May 1884 – 24 May 1979; SS Bessie Self Parker
Parker, James B., 21 Jul 1861 – 4 Mar 1939
Parker, Jimmy G., 17 Jan 1934 – 13 May 1969; SS Thelma Jo Parker
Parker, Thelma Jo, 16 Jan 1940 – [rest of date missing]; SS Jimmy G. Parker
Parker, Walter Frank, 6 Feb 1912 – 25 Mar 1978; SS Florence Lee Parker
Parks, Callie, 1877 – 1950; SS Elick Parks
Parks, Elick, 1868 – 1944; SS Callie Parks
Parks, George, 27 Mar 1913 – 9 Feb 1920
Parks, Hobert, 17 Feb 1906 – 26 Dec 1939
Parks, Joseph E., 28 Jul 1906 – 18 Aug 1984; SS Susie Mae Parks
Parks, Susie Mae, 21 Apr 1908 – 11 May 1991; SS Joseph E. Parks
Parris, Ernestine, 12 May 1933 – 12 May 2000; SS Troy A. Parris; married 31 Jan 1952
Parris, Troy A., 24 Nov 1929 – [rest of date missing]; SS Ernestine Parris; married 31 Jan 1952
Patterson, Bob, 22 Jan 1884 – 8 Jun 1929
Patterson, Harold W., 16 Sep 1924 – 18 Jul 1995; SS Ida Bell Patterson
Patterson, Ida Bell, 17 Mar 1923 – 14 Oct 1992; SS Harold W. Patterson
Patterson, Johnny, 2 Jul 1910 – [rest of date missing]
Patterson, Lee, 13 Apr 1861 – 1 Jul 1943
Patterson, Wilma, 24 Dec 1904 – 30 Jun 1942
Patterson, Winfred Lee, 6 Aug 1927 – 9 Oct 1993; US Army, WWII
Payne, Fred N., 25 Oct 1927 – [rest of date missing]; SS Margaret V. Payne; married 23 Jul 1949
Payne, Margaret V., 5 Mar 1931 – 7 Apr 1996; SS Fred N. Payne; married 23 Jul 1949
Peeples, C. Lonis, 22 Oct 1884 – 18 Jun 1972; SS Ollie L. Peeples
Peeples, Ollie L., 16 Sep 1891 – 3 Sep 1981; SS C. Lonis Peeples
Perkins, Mary Lee, 30 Oct 1887 – 29 Nov 1918
Perry, Bernice V., 24 Sep 1907 – 3 Feb 2002
Pettit, Vesta, daughter of E.D. and F.A. Pettit, 15 Jul 1889 – 22 Oct 1891
Phillips, Alma Norris, 9 Jul 1910 – 18 Sep 1993; SS Fred Phillips
Phillips, Charles Fred, 13 Jun 1902 – 14 Apr 1965; SS Ossie Opal Phillips
Phillips, Elbert B., 5 Mar 1899 – 4 Oct 1957
Phillips, Esther K., 1908 – 1989; SS Troy A. Phillips
Phillips, Fred, 14 Jun 1901 – 12 Feb 1986; SS Alma Norris Phillips
Phillips, G.M., 6 Feb 1930 – [rest of date missing]
Phillips, Grover M., 25 Aug 1889 – 22 Jul 1966; SS Tura Saye Phillips
Phillips, Levi B., 1861 – 1938
Phillips, Loyd S., 8 Feb 1914 – 13 Oct 1977; SS Ruby C. Phillips
Phillips, Mable Clay, 31 Mar 1912 – [rest of date missing]
Phillips, Ollie Elizabeth, 1 Jul 1878 – 31 Mar 1952
Phillips, Ossie Opal, 14 Oct 1908 – 27 Dec 1989; SS Charles Fred Phillips
Phillips, Rex L., 7 May 1901 – 14 Apr 1975; SS Verner Phillips
Phillips, Robert C. "Jack," 12 Mar 1907 – 28 Feb 1986; Masonic emblem; SS Mable Clay Phillips
Phillips, Ruby C., 18 Apr 1911 – 16 Jan 1996; SS Loyd S. Phillips
Phillips, Troy A., 1905 – 1975; SS Esther K. Phillips
Phillips, Tura Saye, 9 Mar 1890 – 10 Jul 1968; SS Grover M. Phillips
Phillips, Verner, 24 Jul 1900 – 2 Apr 1968; SS Rex L. Phillips
Phillips, Virginia L., 31 Jan 1874 – 2 Feb 1959

Poe, Ann B., 31 May 1918 – 4 Jun 1987; SS L.D. Poe
Poe, Ben Raymond, 16 May 1940 – 27 Feb 1991
Poe, Billy, 17 Sep 1948 – 30 Nov 1948
Poe, Chris C., 30 Aug 1917 – 22 Feb 2000; SS Esther M. Poe
Poe, Elmer, 1909 – 1948; SS Lila Poe
Poe, Esther M., 6 Dec 1922 – [rest of date missing]; SS Chris C. Poe
Poe, Geraldine, 20 Aug 1936 – 20 Mar 1985
Poe, L.D., 30 Jul 1911 – 12 Nov 1988; SS Ann B. Poe
Poe, Lila, 1909 – 1943; SS Elmer Poe
Poe, Wesley L., 5 Apr 1937 – 25 Nov 1982, BT US Navy
Powell, Floyd, 31 Mar 1911 – 2 Apr 1941
Powell, Jesse, 21 Dec 1913 – 9 Aug 1975
Powell, Marvin Thomas, 1 Dec 1917 – 24 Feb 1985
Prickett, James F., 5 Aug 1892 – 24 Apr 1945; Masonic emblem; SS Ola Miller Prickett
Prickett, Ola Miller, 17 Aug 1901 – 22 Nov 1985; SS James F. Prickett
Prickett, Sarah A., 12 Feb 1857 – 20 Jan 1923
Prince, Nellie Joe, 5 Sep 1922 – 8 Aug 1924
Pruett, Bumon, 7 Dec 1922 – [rest of date missing]; SS Jewell Pruett
Pruett, Jewell, 25 Dec 1924 – 11 May 1987; SS Bumon Pruett
Pruett, W. Boyd, 17 Jan 1926 – 20 Dec 1991; US Army, WWII
Ragan, E.M., 12 Feb 1867 – 5 Jan 1927
Ragan, Ila Leola Orr, wife of E.M. Ragan 14 Mar 1871 – 15 Oct 1909, [broken monument]
Ramey, Evie Frasier, 20 Feb 1905 – 4 Jan 1985
Rankin, A.L., 14 Feb 1875 – 22 Jul 1929; Masonic emblem; SS N.E. Rankin
Rankin, N.E., 28 Feb 1879 – 19 Nov 1971; SS A.L. Rankin
Rasberry, Melford R., 8 Jan 1888 – 31 May 1947; Alabama Pvt 130 Field Arty 35 Div, WWI
Ray, James R., 1877 – [date date never inscribed]; SS Mary Lizzie Ray
Ray, Mary Lizzie, 1881 – 1933; SS James R. Ray
Ray, Vernie, son of J.R. and M.L. Ray; 3 Apr 1905 – 27 Jun 1921
Reavis, Addie A., wife of J.P. Reavis, 15 Sep 1873 – 22 Aug 1909, [Addie A. Ellison married James P. Reavis 27 Dec 1891, Blount County]
Reavis, B.W., 13 May 1845 – 18 Jan 1919 [Private in Phillips' Legion Georgia Cavalry, CSA; Alabama Confederate Pension Application]
Reavis, Earnest P., son of J.P. and Addie A. Reavis, 14 Dec 1895 – 29 Mar 1917; Co F 4th Ala. Inf., died in U.S. service at Nogalas, Arizona
Reavis, J.P., 10 Aug 1872 – 25 Jul 1930, [James P. Reavis married Addie A. Ellis 27 Dec 1891, Blount County]
Reavis, Mary V., wife of B.W. Reavis, 17 Apr 1848 – 30 Mar 1929
Reed, Florence Josephine, 27 Dec 1877 – 15 Jan 1962; SS J.C. Reed, Sr.
Reed, J.C., Jr., 12 Feb 1918 – 13 Feb 1919
Reed, J.C., Sr., 25 Dec 1875 – 29 May 1940, Masonic emblem; SS Florence Josephine Reed
Reed, Jessie May, 4 Feb 1904 – 29 Feb 1904
Reed, Willie Mitchell, 9 Nov 1901 – 3 Feb 1904
Reed, Wilma Louise, 12 Mar 1914 – 17 May 1916
Reid, Louie E., Dr., 1883 – 1918; SS Sally M. Reid
Reid, Mary A., 21 May 1838 – 4 Jul 1926
Reid, Sally M., 1879 – 1930; SS Dr. Louie E. Reid
Reid, William E., 1860 – 1929
Renfroe, Carol Lynn, 15 Mar 1968 – 21 Feb 1990
Rickles, Annie L., 29 Mar 1872 – 26 Jan 1931; SS Jasper N. Rickles
Rickles, Jasper N., 23 Jun 1865 – 7 Jan 1949; SS Annie L. Rickles
Riddlespur, Jack, [name only, no dates recorded]
Riddlespur, Mary Lee, [name only no dates recorded]
Robberson, Jack D., 19 Jan 1924 – 16 Sep 1985; SS Jessie L. Robberson
Robberson, Jessie L., 31 Jan 1930 – 15 Oct 1975; SS Jack D. Robberson
Robbins, Charlie B., 11 May 1881 – 13 Aug 1960; SS Reeta M. Robbins
Robbins, Edward Marvin, 28 Jun 1870 – 23 Oct 1965; SS Jettie Whatley Robbins
Robbins, Edward, Sr., 1800 – 1864; Private in Company C of the Alabama Mounted Volunteers, Indian Wars, CSA, "In Memory Of"
Robbins, Jettie Whatley, 11 Sep 1881 – 28 Feb 1919; SS Edward Marvin Robbins
Robbins, Lillian F., daughter of W.M. and M.L. Robbins, 7 Aug 1867 – 25 Oct 1905

Robbins, Margaret Marie, 12 Feb 1930 – 27 Feb 1930
Robbins, Mary Wood, 4 Dec 1839 – 11 Feb 1925
Robbins, Reeta M., 20 Jun 1891 – 4 Jan 1990; SS Charlie B. Robbins
Robbins, Shelton, 1824 – 1863; 1st Sergeant of Company K of the 1st Texas Mounted Volunteers, Mexican War, CSA "In Memory Of"
Robbins, William Moore, 24 Jan 1834 – 18 Jul 1913
Roberson, Clara A., 9 Oct 1902 – 9 Nov 1998
Russell, H.H., 10 Dec 1861 – 7 Dec 1925
Samuel, Daniel M., 27 Dec 1851 – 15 Sep 1929
Samuel, Mary E., 26 Mar 1851 – 23 Apr 1919
Sanford, Bessie M., 4 Jul 1907 – 30 May 1989
Sanford, Matt, Jr., 18 Nov 1906 – 31 Dec 1972
Sartin, Alfred V., 5 Mar 1937 – [rest of date missing]; SS Ardith V. Sartin; married 13 Sep 1956
Sartin, Ardith V., 13 Aug 1936 – 14 Aug 1995; SS Alfred V. Sartin; married 13 Sep 1956
Sartin, Idell M. Towe, 21 Jan 1923 – 31 Mar 1987
Saye, [surname only carved on large flat concrete slab]
Saye, Clifford J., 7 Jul 1897 – 8 May 1974; SS Tina J. Saye
Saye, Tina J., 28 Jan 1903 – 18 Dec 1987; SS Cliford J. Saye
Scott, Bettie B., 9 Sep 1882 – 3 Apr 1963; SS Ernest E. Scott
Scott, Ella R., 8 May 1873 – 26 Jan 1963; SS L.B. Scott
Scott, Ernest E., 13 Sep 1880 – 21 Apr 1962; SS Bettie B. Scott
Scott, Ira Eugene, 17 Jan 1877 – 8 Jul 1957
Scott, L.B., 20 Oct 1872 – 11 Jun 1924; SS Ella R. Scott
Scott, Maruice, son of L.B. and E.J. Scott, 19 Oct 1902 –18 Sep 1921
Scott, Willis E., 1898 – 1945
Scruggs, James B., 4 Sep 1895 – 23 Jul 1966; SS Pearl Cain Scruggs
Scruggs, Pearl Cain, 26 Sep 1904 – 14 Apr 1987; SS James B. Scruggs
Seabolt, Shirlee Thompson, 15 Jun 1934 – 18 Apr 2000
Self, Angus E., 16 Jun 1890 – 15 Sep 1945; SS Bessie M. Self
Self, Bessie M., 2 Apr 1895 – 26 Jan 1945; SS Angus E. Self
Self, David Eugene, 20 Nov 1953 – 26 Aug 1972
Self, E. Hewitt, 9 Apr 1896 – 11 May 1966; SS Ruth H. Self
Self, Esto Mae, 6 May 1892 – 24 Apr 1970; SS Robert E. Self
Self, Hermon Morgan, 22 Jan 1923 – 5 Mar 1990; PFC US Army, WWII; SS Mary A. Self
Self, Margaret Sue, 16 Jun 1918 – [rest of date missing]; SS Robert (Bobby) Self
Self, Mary A., 30 Aug 1929 – [rest of date missing]; SS Hermon M. Self
Self, Mattie, wife of W.B. Self, 14 Mar 1866 – 6 Sep 1926
Self, Mayola, 31 Dec 1916 – 27 Mar 1986; SS Walter Self
Self, Mona, 2 Feb 1915 – 9 Aug 1986; SS W. Eugene Self
Self, Phearon, 8 Mar 1919 – 3 Nov 1999; US Coast Guard, WWII
Self, Robert (Bobby), 6 Dec 1914 – 11 Apr 1976; SS Margaret Sue Self
Self, Robert E., 20 Nov 1887 – 28 Mar 1971; SS Esto Mae Self
Self, Ruth H., 21 Nov 1896 – 2 May 1991; SS E. Hewitt Self
Self, Samuel Louis, 22 Jan 1920 – 10 Apr 1972; Masonic emblem
Self, Stephen "Steve" Hermon, 1 Aug 1953 – 27 Sep 1985
Self, W. Eugene, 31 May 1898 – 25 Jun 1979; SS Mona Self
Self, W.B., 13 Apr 1866 – 2 Nov 1939
Self, Walter, 15 Jul 1902 – 22 Dec 1989; SS Mayola Self
Self, Zelma, wife of Eugene Self, 1902 – 1933
Shelton, Coy, 5 Dec 1896 – 18 Sep 1974; SS Irene Shelton
Shelton, Irene, 24 Feb 1900 – 5 Feb 1980; SS Coy Shelton
Shotts, Josephine Freeman, 2 Oct 1915 – [rest of date missing]; SS Ralph Leon Shotts; married 14 May 1936
Shotts, Ralph Leon, 29 May 1913 – 28 Feb 2000; Masonic emblem; SS Josephine Freeman Shotts; married 14 May 1936
Silor, J.D., 25 Jul 1909 – 24 Jan 1941
Simmons, Myra Jo Cummings, 10 Dec 1914 – 9 Jan 1991
Sitz, Audrey J., 7 Mar 1926 – [rest of date missing]; SS Winford Sitz
Sitz, Terry M., 11 Mar 1951 – [rest of date missing]
Sitz, Winford, 4 Apr 1923 – 22 Jun 2000; SS Audrey J. Sitz
Sloan, Allie Mae, 1894 – 1988; SS Victor B. Sloan

Sloan, Bob L., 1931 – 1954
Sloan, Hugh B., 5 Nov 1919 – 25 Jan 1985; Sgt US Army, WWII
Sloan, Hugh T., 1885 – 1952; SS Lillie M. Sloan
Sloan, James P., 22 Dec 1911 – 23 Jan 1976; SS Ruth B. Sloan
Sloan, Lillie M., 1888 – 1982; SS Hugh T. Sloan
Sloan, Oliver J., 16 Nov 1904 – 6 May 1985; SS Vera E. Sloan
Sloan, Ruth B., 9 Mar 1913 – [rest of date missing]; SS James P. Sloan
Sloan, Vera E., 3 Jan 1906 – 5 Feb 1997; SS Oliver J. Sloan
Sloan, Victor B., 1892 – 1945; SS Allie Mae Sloan
Sloan, Virginia, 22 Jun 1924 – 22 Sep 1940
Smith, Bertha R., daughter of J.W. and Ethel Smith, born and died 10 Jan 1927
Smith, Bryan Keith, 1 Feb 1967 – 2 May 1986; PV2 US Army
Smith, Christine D., 16 Jan 1928 – 28 Apr 1992; SS Floyd A. Smith
Smith, Dorothy Cole, wife of Ralph Smith, 28 Jul 1921 – 2 Jan 1943
Smith, Edward W., 7 Oct 1907 – 12 May 1987; SS Willie B. Smith
Smith, Ellen, 21 Feb 1896 – 31 Dec 1978
Smith, Floyd A., 4 May 1932 – [rest of date missing]; SS Christine D. Smith
Smith, Jo Ann, daughter of E.W. and Willie Smith, 15 Sep 1934 – 7 Apr 1935
Smith, Louise Daugette, 26 Feb 1933 – 30 Jul 2002; SS Merman Ray Smith; married 9 Jul 1950
Smith, Merman Ray, 16 May 1930 – 16 Jun 1998; SS Louise Daugette Smith; married 9 Jul 1950
Smith, Ruby May Walker Langley, 9 May 1920 – 6 Aug 1999
Smith, Willie B., 1 Mar 1917 – [rest of date missing]; SS Edward W. Smith
Snead, Curt O., 27 Nov 1899 – 5 Feb 1987; SS Ida Bell Snead
Snead, Ida Bell, 30 Apr 1907 – 20 Mar 1997; SS Curt O. Snead
Snead, Liller, 15 Mar 1894 – 27 Nov 1986
Solley, Lillian B., 28 Aug 1900 – 25 Aug 1991; SS W. Hershell Solley
Solley, W. Hershell, 11 May 1899 – 5 Jun 1973; SS Lillian B. Solley
Solomon, Lettie A., 1 May 1910 – 15 Jun 1988
Spelce, Clyde W., 31 Aug 1911 – 23 Jan 1981; SS Mary Ruth Spelce; married 30 Jul 1955
Spelce, Jeffery, died 1958
Spelce, Larry Dale, died 1946
Spelce, Lillie Mae, 20 Feb 1930 – 4 Jun 1997; SS Lowell Spelce, Jr.
Spelce, Lowell B., 1 Mar 1908 – 31 Mar 1979; SS Mozelle C. Spelce
Spelce, Lowell, Jr., 26 Mar 1928 – 24 Apr 2001; SS Lillie Mae Spelce
Spelce, Mary Ruth, 7 Aug 1934 – [rest of date missing]; SS Clyde W. Spelce; married 30 Jul 1955
Spelce, Mozelle C., 24 Jun 1909 – 14 Mar 1993; SS Lowell B. Spelce
Spivey, Roy B., 27 Oct 1915 – 23 Feb 1968; Alabama, Pvt Btry B 13 Coast Arty
Spivey, Vera Johnston, 11 Aug 1914 – 9 Nov 1989, "Mother of Frances, Jean, Talmadge, Neal"
Sprayberry, Neva T., 9 Oct 1920 – [rest of date missing]; SS William Glen Sprayberry
Sprayberry, William Glen, 18 Jun 1915 – 19 Jun 1992; SS Neva T. Sprayberry
Spurling, Henry, 25 Dec 1874 – 12 Mar 1939
Spurling, Marona, 27 Jan 1908 – 22 Oct 1967; Alabama, Pvt US Marine Corps, WWII; SS Willie Mae Spurling
Spurling, Rosie Lee, 19 Jan 1884 – 17 Sep 1970
Spurling, Roy Dean, 23 Mar 1940 – 26 Mar 1940
Spurling, Willie Mae, 18 Apr 1912 – 6 Jan 1998; SS Marona Spurling
Stanfield, Addie Elgin, 26 Oct 1875 – 12 Jul 1952; SS David B. Stanfield
Stanfield, Alonzo, 1884 – 1934; SS Sarah Stanfield
Stanfield, Audra Self, 5 Sep 1914 – [rest of date missing]; SS Tunis H. Stanfield
Stanfield, David B., 2 Jun 1871 – 25 Apr 1947; SS Addie Elgin Stanfield
Stanfield, Grady E., 31 Oct 1912 – 21 Jun 2000; SS Lucille E. Stanfield; married 29 Oct 1938
Stanfield, Lucille E., 23 Mar 1913 – 22 Dec 1999; SS Grady E. Stanfield; married 29 Oct 1938
Stanfield, Sarah, 1887 – 1969; SS Alonzo Stanfield
Stanfield, Tunis H., 22 Jul 1909 – 28 Feb 1989; SS Audra Self Stanfield
Staton, Ida Lee, 31 Jul 1889 – 28 Oct 1975; SS James Henry Staton
Staton, Infant, of Mr. and Mrs. J.H. Staton, born and died 29 Oct 1916
Staton, James Henry, 29 Mar 1883 – 17 Sep 1953; SS Ida Lee Staton
Staton, Sanders, son of J.H. and Ida Staton, 20 Jun 1911 – 11 Nov 1919
Stewart, T.C. Cheaves, 6 May 1912 – 19 Sep 1981

Stiphens, Elizabeth, 3 Feb 1882 (?) – 27 Mar 1904, [Stephens is spelled with an "i" on this monument; monument is broken, birth date is best guess]
Stonicher, James Henry, 3 May 1914 – 30 Aug 1985; Cpl US Army Air Corps, WWII; SS Mary Frances Smith Stonicher
Stonicher, Mary Frances Smith, 1 Aug 1924 – 21 Jan 1965; SS James Henry Stonicher
Stover, James N., 16 Dec 1891 – 25 Oct 1970; SS Luna D. Stover
Stover, Luna D., 26 Mar 1898 – 20 Jul 1963; SS James N. Stover
Sullivan, Annie, 29 Jun 1876 – 11 Mar 1955; SS Phelan Sullivan
Sullivan, Elbert F., 1 Nov 1889 – 6 Aug 1965; Alabama Pvt US Army, WWI
Sullivan, Ida Brown, 27 Apr 1915 – 13 Oct 1994; SS John Frank Sullivan
Sullivan, J. Ralph, 1882 – 1965; Masonic emblem; SS Kate E. Sullivan
Sullivan, John Frank, 10 Aug 1912 – 25 Dec 1989; SS Ida Brown Sullivan
Sullivan, Kate E., 14 Apr 1893 – 9 Dec 1980; SS J. Ralph Sullivan
Sullivan, Phelan, 12 Dec 1871 – 16 Apr 1962; Masonic emblem; SS Annie Sullivan
Sullivan, Ralph E., 30 Sep 1917 – 27 May 1927
Summers, Cynthia Ann, 1855 – 1947; SS P.M. Summers
Summers, P.M., 1846 – 1932; Masonic emblem; SS Cynthia Ann Summers
Summers, W.F., died Apr 1911, aged 53 years
Summerville, Elva, 6 Jul 1919 – [rest of date missing]; SS Homer T. Summerville
Summerville, Homer T., 10 Jun 1911 – 9 Jan 1989; SS Elva Summerville
Tarrance, Micheal K., 10 Sep 1984 – 10 Sep 1984
Taylor, Edna Couey, 11 May 1916 – 16 Sep 1975
Taylor, Ethel, daughter of Lonnie and Nora Taylor, 3 Nov 1919 – 12 Dec 1917
Taylor, Fannie L., 20 May 1887 – 20 Jun 1955
Taylor, Georgia M., 6 Apr 1890 – 10 Oct 1971
Taylor, James A., son of L.T. and Nora Taylor, 14 Jan 1914 – 10 Jun 1915
Taylor, James Andrew Osgood, 19 Jun 1850 – 21 Dec 1927
Taylor, Lonnie Thomas, 9 Aug 1883 – 10 Feb 1934
Taylor, Margaret Texana Hipp, 6 Feb 1863 – 4 Jan 1945
Taylor, R. Reno, 1879 – 1963
Taylor, Violet Matilda, 4 Nov 1892 – 7 Aug 1907
Teele, J. Lee, 27 Sep 1894 – 8 Jun 1973; SS Myrtie W. Teele
Teele, Myrtie W., 22 Oct 1896 – 17 Aug 1971; SS J. Lee Teele
Thomas, Bertha Cummings, 4 Jul 1910 – 22 Aug 1990; SS Millard "Rube" Thomas
Thomas, Dewey F., 2 Dec 1899 – 10 May 1970; SS Thelma O. Thomas
Thomas, Millard "Rube," 15 Aug 1904 – 27 Feb 1988; SS Bertha Cummings Thomas
Thomas, R.L., 14 Mar 1878 – 14 Feb 1959; SS Sallie Thomas
Thomas, Sallie, 12 Sep 1882 – 4 Nov 1956; SS R.L. Thomas
Thomas, Thelma O., 18 Apr 1918 – [rest of date missing]; SS Dewey F. Thomas
Thompson, A.D., son of J.F. and Nora Thompson, 12 Jul 1913 – 1 Dec 1929
Thompson, Alma, 17 Feb 1904 – 1 Aug 1997
Thompson, Alvin D., 22 Apr 1848 – 28 Oct 1909
Thompson, Alvin, 29 Nov 1929 – 9 Dec 1930
Thompson, Drexel O., 6 Jul 1911 – 17 Nov 1988
Thompson, Earl, 19 Oct 1900 – 8 Jan 1978
Thompson, Elizabeth, 19 Jul 1921 – 17 Jun 1923
Thompson, Emeline, 31 Mar 1855 – 15 Jun 1935; SS L. Pink Thompson
Thompson, Ida Mae, 24 Feb 1892 – 11 Sep 1960; SS William Emmett Thompson
Thompson, J. Freeman, 22 Dec 1874 – 16 Jun 1974
Thompson, J.L., 8 Oct 1916 – 19 Nov 1930
Thompson, John, 13 Dec 1888 – 10 Jun 1970; SS Myrtle Thompson
Thompson, L. Pink, 28 Dec 1852 – 6 Mar 1930; SS Emeline Thompson
Thompson, Martha Carolyn Self, 15 Apr 1930 – 16 Mar 1997
Thompson, Mattie McAfee, 18 Jan 1907 – 9 Mar 2001; SS Milford Hayes Thompson
Thompson, Michael Ray, 30 Jan 1947 – [rest of date missing]; SS Patricia Gail Thompson; married 28 Mar 1967
Thompson, Milford Hayes "Bud," Jr., 29 Dec 1927 – 29 Jan 1998; US Navy, WWII; US Army, Korea
Thompson, Milford Hayes "Tommy," III, 6 Sep 1955 – 6 Aug 2002
Thompson, Milford Hayes, 20 Jan 1903 – 11 Jul 1970; SS Mattie McAfee Thompson
Thompson, Myrtle, 28 Apr 1895 – [rest of date missing]; SS John Thompson

Thompson, Nora L., 23 Jul 1884 – 8 Jan 1949
Thompson, Patricia Gail, 29 Jun 1949 – [rest of date missing]; SS Michael Ray Thompson; married 28 Mar 1967
Thompson, S.M., 9 Dec 1851 – 25 Aug 1925; SS Sue Thompson
Thompson, Sue, 12 Jan 1866 – 30 Aug 1943; SS S.M. Thompson
Thompson, William Emmett, 20 Feb 1890 – 18 Jul 1960; SS Ida Mae Thompson
Tidwell, [surname only on homemade concrete monument]
Tidwell, Nathan L., 29 Nov 1873 – 4 Jan 1941; SS Retta A. Tidwell
Tidwell, Retta A., 24 Dec 1883 – 22 Aug 1964; SS Nathan L. Tidwell
Tidwell, William Andrew, 23 Mar 1900 – 2 Oct 1937
Tilley, Vester Watts, 16 Jul 1919 – 20 Apr 1983
Timm, Audie Mae, 6 Apr 1929 – 7 Sep 1985; SS Dallas Timm
Timm, Dallas, 17 Jan 1916 – 9 Sep 1999; SS Audie Mae Timm
Towe, Ernest, 3 Jun 1916 – 6 Sep 1978; S1 US Navy, WWII
Turner, A.B., 6 Oct 1869 – 4 Jan 1931
Turner, Alice, wife of A.B. Turner, 1 Nov 1875 – 8 Nov 1908
Turner, Arizona Durham, 18 Jun 1866 – 22 Mar 1949
Turner, Claud A., 12 Oct 1903 – 16 Jun 1968; SS Nellie B. Turner
Turner, Curtis E., 28 Sep 1897 – 24 Aug 1976; SS Frankie R. Turner
Turner, Frankie R., 13 Mar 1898 – 12 Jul 1983; SS Curtis E. Turner
Turner, Georgia, 16 Mar 1876 – 7 Aug 1961; SS James W. Turner
Turner, Gloria, [no dates recorded, possible plot marker]
Turner, James W., 18 Jan 1874 – 31 Jan 1940; SS Georgia Turner
Turner, Jennifer Ann, 6 Apr 1990 – 16 Dec 1995
Turner, Margaret N., [no dates recorded, possible plot marker]
Turner, Mary A., [no dates recorded, possible plot marker]
Turner, Mary D., 12 Oct 1844 – 24 Apr 1914; SS Preston C. Turner
Turner, Nellie B., 8 Sep 1907 – 19 May 1985; SS Claud A. Turner
Turner, Preston C., 9 Feb 1847 – 6 Apr 1916; SS Mary D. Turner
Turner, Stella Mozelle, daughter of A.B. and Alice Turner, 5 May 1894 – 19 Sep 1896
Underwood, Maggie Margaret, 29 Sep 1892 – 8 Oct 1984
Vandiver, Alice Gash, 1871 – 1940; SS James Z. Vandiver
Vandiver, Anna Mae, 18 May 1903 – 18 Jan 1990; SS Nellie J. Vandiver
Vandiver, Irene H., 17 Oct 1921 – 8 Jan 1993; SS J.C. Vandiver; married 27 Dec 1939
Vandiver, J.C., 21 Dec 1916 – [rest of date missing]; SS Irene H. Vandiver; married 27 Dec 1939
Vandiver, James Z., 1868 – 1950; SS Alice Gash Vandiver
Vandiver, Nellie J., 23 Aug 1905 – 21 Jun 1997; SS Anna Mae Vandiver
Vaughn, David L., 8 Jan 1966 – 9 Jan 1966
Vaughn, Dovie, 5 Dec 1889 – 23 May 1914
Vaughn, Everette, 17 Mar 1912 – 11 Sep 1929
Vernon, Bertha Dillard, 31 Oct 1912 – 21 Jul 1993
Vernon, Cornelia Wilson, 25 May 1876 – 1 Nov 1961; SS James Oscar Vernon
Vernon, James Oscar, 25 May 1875 – 18 Sep 1950; SS Cornelius Wilson Vernon
Vernon, Joe, 15 Mar 1933 – 5 Jan 1997; CWO2 US Navy
Vernon, Martha Jo, 7 Oct 1937 – 24 Feb 2000
Vernon, Ralph Edward, 29 Apr 1903 – 18 Dec 1963
Vickery, Geneva W., 1918 – [rest of date missing]; SS Rabon R. Vickery
Vickery, Rabon R., 1914 – 1994; SS Geneva W. Vickery
Visage, Lela N., 17 Feb 1900 – [rest of date missing]; SS R.L. Visage
Visage, Roudey L., 19 Dec 1895 – 18 Jan 1972; Georgia, Pvt US Army, WWI; SS Lela N. Visage
Wade, Victor, 28 Jun 1872 – 29 Jan 1935
Wade, Zula, daughter of William Young, 1875 – 1913
Waid, Betty E., wife of J.C. Waid, 25 Apr 1870 – 18 Oct 1943
Waid, Eli, 1 Oct 1875 – 7 Aug 1937
Waid, Ellender S., daughter of Eli and Elizabeth Glover and wife of J.C. Waid, 14 May 1852 – 20 Feb 1892
Waid, Georgia A., wife of J.C. Waid, daughter of W.A. Harris, 19 Oct 1871 – 19 Mar 1926, [Georgia A. Harris married James C. Waid, Jr. 10 Aug 1891, Blount County]
Waid, Girdie, daughter of J.C. and B.E. Waid, 2 Jun 1896 – 19 Sep 1905
Waid, J.C., 18 May 1847 – 22 Jun 1920, [James C. Waid, Jr. married Georgia A. Harris 10 Aug 1891, Blount County]
Waid, Laila, 6 Dec 1893 – 30 Nov 1912; SS Lessie Waid

Waid, Lessie, 19 Sep 1895 – 1 Sep 1912; SS Laila Waid
Walker, Bishop K., Sr., 8 Feb 1890 – 1 Feb 1978; Masonic emblem; SS Grace D. Walker
Walker, Grace D., 25 Feb 1893 – 2 Apr 1976; SS Bishop K. Walker, Sr.
Walker, Harold Wallace, 21 Sep 1921 – 12 May 1923
Walker, Joseph Wilson, 14 Jun 1917 – 12 Aug 1919
Walls, Ernest G., 2 Aug 1912 – 17 Dec 1992; S2 US Navy, WWII; SS Verna M. Walls; married 11 Jan 1936
Walls, Verna M., 19 Mar 1919 – 3 Mar 1996; SS Ernest G. Walls; married 11 Jan 1936
Ward, Joseph H., 30 Jan 1875 – 18 Feb 1956; SS Susan A. Ward
Ward, Susan A., 23 Aug 1883 – 21 Dec 1955; SS Joseph H. Ward
Watts, Arthur T., 12 Jul 1901 – 1 Nov 1967
Webb, Edna L., 1 Nov 1911 – 24 Jun 1981
Webb, George, 24 Feb 1879 – 24 May 1967; SS Pearl Webb
Webb, Pearl, 23 Jul 1884 – 2 Jun 1951; SS George Webb
Whatley, Jettie, wife of E.M. Robbins, born Ennis, Texas 11 Sep 1881 – 28 Feb 1919
Wheeler, Marie Anderson, 19 Apr 1920 – 21 Mar 1987
Whidby, Constance Lynn, 29 Oct 1961 – 18 May 1995
Whisenant, [surname only on homemade concrete monument; two separate monument, one is broken]
White, Alline, daughter of W.D. and F.B. White, 7 Jul 1905 – 10 Jul 1906
White, Fannye Williams, 21 Jul 1876 – 11 Feb 1953; SS William David White
White, H.L., 1865 – 1945; SS Ida N. White
White, Harold Lee, 17 Aug 1911 – 29 Jan 1996; Masonic emblem; SS Mary Bradford White
White, Hellice M., 28 Jul 1924 – [rest of date missing]; SS William G. White
White, Ida N., 1868 – 1958; SS H.L. White
White, James Russell, 22 Aug 1914 – 22 Jul 1989; SS Madeline Faust White
White, Madeline Faust, 13 May 1919 – 31 Aug 1978; SS James Russell White
White, Mary Bradford, 15 Jun 1917 – 15 Aug 2000; SS Harold Lee White
White, Susan, wife of R.B. White, 3 Aug 1859 – 31 May 1902
White, William David, 1 Jun 1876 – 4 Dec 1960; SS Fannye Williams White
White, William Gurley, 25 Mar 1921 – 30 Apr 1994; TSgt US Army, WWII; SS Hellice M. White
Whitlock, Mildred June, 25 Nov 1924 – 14 Apr 1996
Whitworth, Steven "Tyler," 11 Sep 1990, [only date recorded]
Widner, Bertha V., 19 Dec 1911 – 10 May 1987; SS Samuel D. Widner
Widner, Samuel D., 18 May 1914 – 14 Dec 1982; Pvt US Army; SS Bertha V. Widner
Wilemon, Bobby Grayel, 4 Jun 1933 – 26 Jul 1983; Airman 1st Class
Wilemon, Flora Belle, 8 May 1916 – 1 Jul 1990; SS Verbon Bee Wilemon
Wilemon, Verbon Bee, 7 Aug 1914 – 22 Sep 1980; SS Flora Belle Wilemon
Williams, Claud V., 20 Feb 1888 – 23 Aug 1971; SS Verna Mae Bradford Williams
Williams, Dorothy, 19 Feb 1921 – 26 Jan 2000; SS James L. "J.L." Williams
Williams, Glennie Ruth, 22 Apr 1922 – [rest of date missing]; SS W.B. (Bill) Williams
Williams, James L. "J.L.," 14 May 1916 – 4 Apr 1998; SS Dorothy Williams
Williams, James M., 30 Aug 1860 – 12 Dec 1942; SS Mollie Williams
Williams, Jasper, 20 Oct 1882 – 11 May 1964
Williams, Lillie Mae, wife of C.V. Williams, 28 Jun 1893 – 29 Sep 1912
Williams, Mollie, 19 Sep 1867 – 23 Feb 1937; SS James M. Williams
Williams, Opal, [no dates recorded, homemade concrete monument]
Williams, Thomas W., 4 Feb 1895 – 10 May 1970; Alabama, Pvt Co D 1 Bn Repl Tng Cen, WWI
Williams, Verna Mae Bradford, 22 Jul 1896 – 12 Apr 1958; SS Claud V. Williams
Williams, W.B. (Bill), 16 Aug 1920 – 10 Jul 1988; SS Glennie Ruth Williams
Willingham, Ross, 3 Apr 1914 – 22 Mar 1987
Willis, Frank, Jr., 15 Nov 1923 – 5 Jan 1980; Tec 4 US Army, WWII; SS Opal Weaver Willis; married 31 Mar 1951
Willis, Gregory Thomas, 28 Feb 1955 – 21 Jul 1997
Willis, Opal Weaver, 12 Feb 1925 – 20 Dec 2000; SS Frank Willis, Jr.; married 31 Mar 1951
Wilson, Aria Blain, 1909 – 1987; SS Luther W. Wilson
Wilson, Luther W., 1898 – 1986; SS Aria Blain Wilson
Wilson, Margaret, [no dates recorded, homemade concrete monument]
Wilson, Pink, [no dates recorded, homemade concrete monument]
Wood, Joyce D., 22 Jan 1956 – 5 May 1991; daughter; SS Tommie L. Couey
Works, Grady, 16 Nov 1919 – 26 Sep 1981; Pvt US Army, WWII

Works, Jason, 26 Feb 1973 – 19 Apr 1994
Wright, Emaline, 1887 – 1983; SS J. Marvin Wright
Wright, J. Marvin, 1887 – 1958; SS Emaline Wright
Wright, M. Felton, 4 Oct 1915 – 26 May 1931
Wynn, Allen Baskin, Dr., 11 Jul 1840 – 5 Aug 1916
Wynn, Frank Allen, 30 Jan 1919 – 27 Mar 1993
Wynn, Frank Newton, 14 Feb 1881 – 8 Mar 1951
Wynn, Jessie Dalton, 13 Jan 1889 – 9 Apr 1932
Wynn, Josephine Lawson, 29 Mar 1851 – 4 Jul 1932
Wynn, Mary Emma, 14 Dec 1883 – 5 Aug 1912
Wynn, Roncie Eugene, 26 Dec 1923 – 23 Aug 1934
Yarbrough, Alma, 1886 – 1936
Yates, J.T., 13 Apr 1928 – 30 Dec 1990; SS Ruby Yates
Yates, Ruby, 2 Jul 1929 – 18 Dec 1997; SS J.T. Yates
Young, J.B., 16 Mar 1862 – 13 Jun 1938
Young, Mary E., 23 Jul 1867 – 3 May 1941

-Appendix B-

Altoona Cemetery

Altoona cemetery was deeded on September 19, 1913, by J.W. Rickles and wife Annie Rickles to J.F. Whisenant and W.M. Hurt. The deed states, *"Less than ½ acre in the southeast corner reserved as colored cemetery."* W.A. Lewis says in his book *Little known burial sites and cemeteries of Etowah County Alabama*, that roughly 50 other graves exist with no marker, or just a field stone. Surveyed between 1990-1997.

Adams, Allie, 11 Jan 1910 – 12 Mar 1915; Daughter of John and Leler Adams
Catling, Annie B., 1900-1964
Catling, Charles, 1924-1956
Catling, Limovs, Jr., 1909-1974
Curry, Rev. Pleas, 1884-1968
Findley, James, 15 Jul 1905 - 30 Mar 1950; Masonic Emblem
Garlington, James W., 23 Oct 1927 - 3 Oct 1979; MS3 U.S. Navy, World War II, Korea
Gray, George, 1876 - 26 July 1916; Mosaic Templars of America Emblem
Johnson, Emma Lee, 26 Feb 1910 - 30 Oct 1953
Kidd, Hodie Mae, 20 Dec 1918 - 20 Mar 1920; Daughter of Jesse and Pearl Kidd
Mathis, Richard Jr., 27 Sept. 1947 - 13 May 1997; Precious Lord Take My Hand
Mathis, Patrick Landon, 13 Dec. 1977 - 31 Jan 2008; Son of Richard and Patricia
Moseley, James H., 1929 - 1965
Robinson, Willard, 1919 - 1979; PVT. U.S. Army, World War 2
Tinker, I.V,. 31 Jul 1900 - 16 October 1970
Whetlow, Henry, 10 Jan 1878 – 26 May 1917; Mosaic Templars of America Emblem

Bibliography

63, Altoona Evergreen Chapter. *Altoona Evergreen Chapter 63 Cookbook*. Altoona, Al, 1978.

A.M., Grand Lodge A.F. &. *Proceedings of the Grand Lodge A.F. & A.M. of Alabama*. Montgomery, Alabama: Brown Printing Company, 1908.

—. *Proceedings of the Grand Lodge A.F. & A.M. of Alabama*. Montgomery: Brown Printing Company, 1922.

Alabama, Geological Survey of. *Statistics of the mineral production of Alabama*. Geological Survey of Alabama, 1913, 1916, 1923, 1926, 1929.

Alabama, University Of. *Altoona Population Numbers*. Tuscaloosa, Alabama: University Of Alabama Press, 2008.

Altoona Cash and Record Book. Located in Altoona Town Hall, 1908-1930's.

"Altoona High School Annual." 1957.

Attalla Mirror.n.d.

Bank, Exchange. *Exchange Bank Celebrates 100 Years*. Exchange Bank, 2009.

Bradstreet, Dun &. *Book Of Commercial Ratings*. New York, 1900-1930.

Bureau, U.S. Census. *Altoona, Alabama -American FactFinder*. 2010. http://factfinder2.census.gov/faces/nav/jsf/pages/searchresults.xhtml?refresh=t (accessed April 30, 2012).

Bureau, United States Census. " 9th Federal Census of the United States." 1870.

Castner, Personal Correspondence with Mr. Charles. *Information on L&N Railroad* (September-October 2008).

Co., E.I. Du Pont De Nemours &. *High Explosives: Their Manufacture, Handling, Storage, and Use*. Wilmington, Delaware: DuPont, 1920.

Company, Alabama Mineral Land. "Lands Of The Alabama Mineral Land Company." 1890.

Company, E.I. Du Pint de Nemours &. *High Explosives: Kinds, Grades and Brands*. Wilmington, Delaware: DuPont, 1915.

Contributors to 2008 Centennial, various interview and web sources, Etowah County Historical Society, Eddie Robbins, Personal Photographs. "Picture Credits." n.d.

Crownover, Danny. *Emails From Danny Crownover*. Gadsden, Al, 2008-2010.

Culver, I.F. "Alabama's resources and future prospects, 1897." Birmingham: Roberts & Son, 1897.

"Delorme Topo USA v8." 2009.

Department, Post Office. "Location Of Post Offices." Washington DC.: National Archives Morrow, GA, 1900,1915, 1939,1942.

dictionary.com. *Altoona| Define Altoona at Dictionary.com*. 2010. http://dictionary.reference.com/browse/altoona?jss=1 (accessed March 11, 2010).

DuBose, Joel Campbell. *Notable men of Alabama: personal and genealogical, Volume 2*. Southern Historical Association, 1904.

Farabee, G.L. (Red). *The blessed depression of the '30s*. New York: Vantage, 1976.

Fulton, John. *Coke*. Scranton, Pa: International Textbook Company, 1906.

Gannett, Henry. "Gadsden 30 Minute Quadrangle." USGS, 1885.

Gibson, A.M. *Report on the Raccoon Mountain Coal Field*. Montgomery, Ala: Barrett & Co., State Printers and Binders, 1883.

H.F. Wilson, Jr. "Map of Blount Mountain and Contiguous Areas." Alabama Department of Archives and History, 1893.

Herr, Kincaid. *The Louisville and Nashville Railroad 1850-1942*. Lousisville, Ky: L&N Magazine, August 1943.

History, U.S. Department of Archives and. "Post Office Locations and Postmasters." U.S. Postal Service, n.d.

Ironminers.com. *Iron Miners Forum*. n.d. http://www.ironminers.com/mineforum/viewforum.php?f=19&sid=423c0b3965b08c0f03c9a724fca2a244.

Lewis, William A. *Little known burial sites and cemeteries of Etowah County Alabama*. Gadsden, Al: Self Published, 1997.

Lincoln, F.C. *Coal Washing in Illinois*. Champaign, Illinois: University Of Illinois, October 27, 1913.

Maynor, Eugene. *Maynor Genealogy*. 1983.

McAfee, Juanita. "Looking Back." n.d.

McAfee, Juanita. "My Viewpoint In Bits and Pieces." May 1998.

McCray, Howard, interview by Ryan Cole and Andrew McCray. (2008, 2009).

Nix, Dalton, J. *E-mails with Dalton Nix*. 2007-2010.

Owen, Thomas M. *Alabama Official and Statistical Register* . Montgomery: Department of Archives and History, Brown Publishing Company, 1913.

Patrem, Ann Echols. *Altoona: 1900 to 1989...A Brief History*. Altoona, Alabama, 1989.

Powell, George. "A Description and History of Blount County." *Alabama Historical Quarterly*, 1965: Volume 27, pages 95 -132.

Records, Alabama Secretary Of State Government. *Government Records Inquiry System*. March 2010.

http://www.sos.state.al.us/vb/inquiry/inquiry.aspx?area=Corporations.

sacred-texts.com. *105. The Southern And Western Tribes.* n.d. http://sacred-texts.com/nam/cher/motc/motc105.htm (accessed 2010).

Service, United States Postal. "Postmaster Finder." Janruary 1, 2010. http://webpmt.usps.gov/pmt002.cfm.

Sitz, Terry. *E-mails with Terry Sitz.* 2007.

Society, Alabama High School Football Historical. *Altoona High School Football History.* n.d. http://www.ahsfhs.org/Teams2/teampage.asp?Team=Altoona (accessed April 2010).

Sterling, Robin. "Blount County Alabama Cemeteries Vol. 3." 2005.

Stine, S.B. "Motor-Driven Stine Mine Fan." *Mines and Minerals*, August 1903: 281.

Sultzman, Lee. *Chickasaw.* October 11, 1999. http://tolatsga.org/chick.html.

"Tallman's Map of Etowah County, Alabama." Cincinnati: Krebs Lithographing Co., 1877.

The Gadsden Times. n.d.

The Southern Democrat. n.d.

TNGenWeb, and Fredrick Smoot. *A Walk Through Time: The Chickasaw and Their Cessions.* 1996-2002. http://www.tngenweb.org/tnfirst/chicksaw/walktime.htm.

Tubbs, Bill, and Sue Tubbs. *Blount County, Alabama ancestral homesteads.* Jasper, Ala: B. Tubbs, 1999.

—. *Etowah County, Alabama ancestral homesteads.* Jasper, Ala: B. Tubbs, 2001.

Underwood, Eugene, J.W. Penn, J.N. Rickles, B.H. Ellison, and F.G. Lee. "Altoona Subdivision Plats." Altoona: Etowah County Courthouse, 1905-1913.

Wapedia. *Wapedia - Wiki: Altoona, Pennsylvania.* March 8, 2010. http://wapedia.mobi/en/Altoona,_Pennsylvania (accessed March 11, 2010).

Weather Underground. 2009. http://www.wunderground.com/US/AL/Altoona.html (accessed January 25, 2010).

Wilbert, Kevin. *E-mails with Kevin Wilbert.* 2007-2010.

Wilson, H.F. "Map Of Blount Mountain." University Of Alabama, December 1893.

www.ingramcontent.com/pod-product-compliance
Lightning Source LLC
Chambersburg PA
CBHW080343170426
43194CB00014B/2671

3. Our company employs more than 30,000 people worldwide.

Wh-question: _____
Question tag type 1: _____
Question tag type 2: _____
Yes / No question: _____

4. Susan drives a blue car.

Wh-question: _____
Question tag type 1: _____
Question tag type 2: _____
Yes / No question: _____

5. The British prime minister lives at No. 10 Downing Street.

Wh-question: _____
Question tag type 1: _____
Question tag type 2: _____
Yes / No question: _____

6. We run training sessions every quarter.

Wh-question: _____
Question tag type 1: _____
Question tag type 2: _____
Yes / No question: _____

7. The Great Wall of China is more than 21,000 km long.

Wh-question: _____
Question tag type 1: _____
Question tag type 2: _____
Yes / No question: _____